MAKING DECISIONS IN MULTINATIONAL CORPORATIONS
CORPORATIONS
Managing Relations With
Sovereign Governments

MAKING DECISIONS IN MULTINATIONAL CORPORATIONS
Managing Relations With Sovereign Governments

AMIR MAHINI

Director of International Business Research
McKinsey and Company, Inc.

JOHN WILEY & SONS
New York • Chichester • Brisbane • Toronto • Singapore

Library of Congress Cataloging-in-Publication Data:

Mahini, Amir.
  Making decisions in multinational corporations:
managing relations with sovereign governments
      p.   cm.
  ISBN 0-471-84092-0
  1. International business enterprises—Decision making.
I. Title.
HD62.4.M32   1988   87-37591
658.4′03—dc19   CIP

Printed in the United States of America
10   9   8   7   6   5   4   3   2   1

To my parents

Foreword

By examining the actual practices of a number of multinational enterprises, Dr. Mahini has produced a pioneering work on an important management problem: how firms should organize themselves to handle their relations with governments in the many countries where they operate. The dilemma underlying this decision is faced by all top managers of multinationals and has become increasingly significant with the advent of global competition. Prior to Mahini's study, no researcher had clearly focused on this critical management issue and identified the variables that have led firms to adopt different approaches in managing their relations with foreign governments. Mahini tells us that there are underlying patterns in managers' practice; that, even without clear and explicit rationale, managers have eventually moved toward the approaches that made sense for their firms. Understanding the reasons for the choices of the firms included in this study can help other managers avoid mistakes and move more quickly toward solutions that are workable for their particular enterprises.

Dr. Mahini's interest in the subject began when he encountered, while he was at Harvard Business School, the difficulties, and seemingly original solutions, of one well-known, large, multinational enterprise. The decisions made by the firm seemed to make sense for the enterprise at the particular time; but the recommendations by the company's managers that other firms follow this company's lead made less sense to Dr. Mahini. It seemed to him that there was no "right" approach that would work for all firms at all times. Dr. Mahini saw his task, from the outset, as identifying those characteristics of a particular firm that might influence the approach which that class of firms should take to handle government relations problems. The search was for important underlying patterns.

It should be made clear at the very outset that Dr. Mahini does not try to tell the reader what results a company should seek in its negotiations with governments. Whether a multinational should yield to pressures for local ownership, how much subsidy it should seek when it is considering investing in a particular country, or whether it should export more or less—these are not the topics of this book. Dr. Mahini does talk about how firms ought to go about organizing themselves to make such decisions. Should the decisions be left to the subsidiary manager, for example? Or should top management make such decisions? Or should various levels of management be somehow involved? If various levels, through what organizational framework? This book is on how to structure the firm for negotiation and decision-making; it is not about how to conduct negotiations or what decisions should come out of discussions with governments.

Dr. Mahini tells us that firms face a basic dilemma. That dilemma is similar to the one managers encounter in other areas in allocating decision-making authority: decentralization clearly has its advantages, but centralization also offers real advantages. Although it is not easy to have both sets of advantages, managers sometimes try solutions that lie between the two extremes. In the case of international government relations, leaving authority solely in the hands of managers of overseas subsidiaries certainly has a good deal to be said for it. The favorable points are clearly identified by Mahini, and in some firms they dominate the allocation of decision authority with regard to government relations. On the other hand, there are real gains in centralizing decision-making in multinationals. For some of the firms that Mahini studied, these gains outweighed the very significant costs associated with taking away authority and responsibility from the subsidiary manager. But some of the most interesting firms described in this book are those that tried to walk the fence between the extremes. Mahini tells us how different firms managed this balancing act, and why this tightrope, in spite of its complications, is appropriate for some multinationals.

Dr. Mahini studied in detail the decision-making processes in 13 firms. This is a large number when one realizes the kind of information that had to be collected in a study of a subject about which virtually nothing was known before Mahini started. But the reader will not be overwhelmed by statistical analysis; in fact, there is none. Analysis of 13 firms does not lend itself to statistical techniques. Future researchers will, no doubt, study more firms, in less depth. They will add to our knowledge by including kinds of firms that Dr. Mahini had to ignore: Japanese and European, for example. They will add knowledge about how diversified firms handle the different parts of their enterprises. And they will look at different industries. But all future work in this area must draw on the hypotheses created by Dr. Mahini.

This pioneering research is particularly important for managers. Its rich detail about practices of firms and the accompanying analysis informs managers in ways that can be of genuine help in framing their own decisions. Managers cannot afford the luxury of waiting for the next round of studies with larger samples and sophisticated quantitative techniques. They must make decisions now, and this study offers real help. It does not provide automatic answers; it does provide valuable ways for managers to think about their problems and to design solutions that are appropriate to the needs of their firms.

LOUIS T. WELLS, JR.
Herbert F. Johnson Professor of
    International Management
Harvard Graduate School of
    Business Administration
Boston, Massachusetts

Acknowledgments

Like any research undertaking, mine owes its realization to the cooperation and support of a large number of people and organizations. I wish to express my sincere appreciation to the many managers whom I had the pleasure of interviewing. All of them contributed generously of their time, insights, and experiences.

Much of the research was conducted while I was at the Harvard Business School during the early 1980s. I am deeply indebted to Professors Michael Y. Yoshino, Joseph L. Bower, and Louis T. Wells, Jr. for their invaluable suggestions, contributions, and encouragement. They gave unstintingly of their time and constantly challenged me to be rigorous in my research and practical in my message.

At McKinsey, the importance of getting the relations between multinational corporations and sovereign governments right has been repeatedly driven home to me by my colleagues in the International Management practice. I am especially thankful to Tino Puri and Denis Tinsley for their support and friendship.

I am grateful to Bill Matassoni for constantly encouraging me to bring this book to fruition, and to Bill Price for shepherding the manuscript through numerous editorial and production stages. I thank Katherine Johnson for her contributions during the writing phase; and my editor, John Mahaney, for his patience, support, and understanding.

This book will undoubtedly have its share of shortcomings. For these, I am entirely responsible.

A.M.

Contents

Contents

MAKING DECISIONS IN MULTINATIONAL CORPORATIONS
CORPORATIONS
Managing Relations With
Sovereign Governments

1

Management of Government Relations

Neither the MNC nor the nation-state shows much evidence of losing its vitality in the world economy.

— Raymond Vernon, *Storm Over the Multinationals*, 1977

Multinational corporations (MNCs), whether from the United States or from other countries, must deal with the demands and concerns of various national governments in whose jurisdictions they operate. Government policies toward industrialization may support the MNCs' strategy in serving global markets or they may prove to be the undoing of that strategy. How, and to what extent, are MNCs organized to manage, properly and best, their affairs and their relations with their hosts?

The varied and complex challenges posed by government-related issues are illustrated in the following examples:

The Management Committee of Exxon Corporation is considering a major investment proposal for a petrochemical facility in a large developing country.

During the presentation the Vice President of Exxon's Chemical Division reminds the eight senior corporate executives who make up the Management Committee that the host government is eager to see this plant built and that, as a result, the Chemical Division has steadily increased its commitment to the project over several years.

He informs the committee that the profitability of the project could swing from poor to excellent, depending on the decision about taxes to be made by government authorities who have wide latitute concerning the project. He admits that considerable uncertainty remains regarding the position that the authorities will adopt. When questioned by the Chairman, it is admitted that no good precedent exists but that the country is unlikely to discourage a respectable return on investment. This seems to fall short of allaying the committee's fears.

In the discussion that follows the Chemical Division representatives mince no words: they warn their superiors that if Exxon wants to continue to operate in the region they have little choice but to cooperate with the host country in this proposal. In effect, they argue that Exxon should make the investment not only for the potential profits of the project but with the understanding that the investment will help to protect the larger profits from the company's petroleum operations in the region.

The presentation runs its course. Finally, Garvin, Exxon's Chairman, announces that he does not see anything wrong with the proposal, adding: "I don't know how we are going to do this thing without assuming some risk . . . what's at stake here is not whether we can avoid the risk, but how we are going to deal with the bureaucrats." He pauses and asks for the record: "Well, is everybody in agreement to go ahead with this thing?"

"Anybody know any alternatives?" someone rejoins.[1]

After much pressure a U.S. industrial company agreed to build an additional plant to manufacture certain product

---

[1]Anthony J. Parisi, "Inside Exxon," *The New York Times Magazine*, August 3, 1980.

components in a European country. This decision was made despite the existence of excess capacity in the company's other European plants that produce similar components which could supply this market. Management was aware that from a narrow cost perspective a single supply source for Europe would probably have been the most efficient. It was also aware that the new investment resources required for the project would reduce the pool of resources available for investment elsewhere in the system. Corporate management, however, could not afford to ignore the implicit risk that such a "request" posed to the sales of other product lines in that country for which public agencies and state-owned companies were major customers.

In 1977 IBM was faced with a critical decision on a decade-old Indian government demand to reduce its ownership of local operations to a minority status. Rather than compromise its consistent worldwide policy of 100% ownership and set a precedent for its operations elsewhere in the world, IBM decided to withdraw from India.

A pharmaceutical firm was introducing a major product developed for the first time ever in a European country. It launched a massive advance publicity campaign targeted at doctors and hospitals and announced a release date but could not reach an agreement with the government regarding pricing for the new drug. The price suggested by the government was regarded by the firm as inadequate. Given the important worldwide precedent-setting nature of new drug pricing, the firm was faced with a dilemma. Submitting to the government's price would leave the firm vulnerable to not recovering its large R&D investment; withholding the drug's introduction could result in strained relations with the government and might jeopar-

dize the goodwill of medical professionals who were looking forward to the drug. The firm decided to distribute the
product free, pending agreement with the government on
price. It took 18 months before the government agreed to a
price that the company found acceptable.

These situations are representative of the scores of management
decisions necessitated by the kinds of host-government demands and interventions that multinational companies continually confront and that temper their drives for efficiency and
global competitive advantage.

MULTINATIONAL CORPORATIONS AND NATIONAL GOVERNMENTS

In the United States the debate on the ideological underpin-
nings of government regulation or intervention in business is
now being joined in earnest. Abroad, however, that debate has
long run its course. Overseas, governments have increasingly
come to assume the mantle of national economic managers and
their performance in this role is given great weight by the elec-
torate. As such, whether in the industrialized democracies of
Europe or in the developing economies of Latin America,
Africa, or Asia, governments not only provide the legal and regulatory framework for domestic and foreign business but, to
varying extents, frame and implement national industrial policies. Toward this end they also intervene in specific industrial
sectors and seek to affect individual firms, especially foreign
firms, selectively by tailored regulation or direct negotiations.

The multinational firm as an institution poses a number of
challenges to national government policies. Multinational firms
are constantly engaged in making strategic decisions such as the
location of new investment, flow of intersubsidiary trade, transfer of technology, location of R&D, and whom to employ and
under what conditions—both of which have an impact on and

are affected by government policies. Vernon[2] characterized these challenges as "sovereignty at bay." Barnett and Muller[3] and Behrman,[4] among others, have discussed the issues involved in MNC-national government relations from vastly different ideological perspectives.

The tenor of thought and practice regarding MNCs, originally focused on their benefits and evils as institutions and whether or not to tolerate their presence, has now shifted to the practical realm of how to use them best to further national goals. The attraction of multinationals to host governments is occasioned by such benefits to the national economy as the development of the industrial base, creation of jobs, generation of taxes, and stimulation of secondary activities such as local suppliers and the promise of exports. Host governments are constantly seeking ways in which they can increase the benefits to their economies from foreign investment both at the time of investment by specification of entry conditions and subsequent to the establishment of operations. In doing so they frequently try to influence MNCs on specific issues like increasing local value-added, encouraging exports, maintenance of stable price levels, and the enhancement of national technological capabilities. Some insist on local ownership in MNC operations as a means of ensuring a local say in the strategies and operations of these firms or on political grounds.

Host-government policies place a tremendous demand on MNCs. Host governments seem to expect both responsiveness to their individual national policies and maintenance of international competitiveness. Yet for MNCs, maintaining competi-

[2]Raymond Vernon, *Sovereignty at Bay* (Basic Books, New York, 1971).
[3]Richard T. Barnett and R.E. Muller, *Global Reach, The Power of the Multinational Corporations* (Simon & Schuster, New York, 1974).
[4]Jack N. Behrman, *U.S. International Business and Governments* (McGraw-Hill, New York, 1971). See also John Fayerweather (Ed.), *International Business-Government Affairs, Toward an Era of Accommodation* (Ballinger, Cambridge, MA, 1973). For a review of many issues involved in the debate see T.J. Bierstecker, *Distortion or Development? Contending Perspectives on the Multinational Corporation* (MIT Press, Cambridge, MA, 1979).

tiveness on a global scale often conflicts with being responsive to national policies. Making their activities more interdependent across countries to enhance economic competitiveness, for instance, allows MNCs less flexibility in responding to the policies of any individual country. It is clear that MNCs must recognize government demands or "political imperatives" as additional sources of complexity in choosing business strategies, designing organizations, and running operations.

The consequences of nonmanagement or mismanagement of government relations for MNCs can be serious. Some scholars of international business have warned that competitive success in the 1980s may be determined more by the ability to construct a corporate technology of international government-relations management than by the traditional performance criteria of the marketplace.[5] Bower and Doz,[6] in summarizing the problems that confront top management of a multinational in handling the contradictory demands inherent in managing diversity on the one hand and interdependence on the other, emphasize the importance of government relations:

> Aggravating the difficulty facing top management is the desire of virtually all governments in the world to sit at the managing committee table and influence the locus of power. In almost every situation, the desired balance of administrative rationality contradicts the demands of political acceptability. Or, if for purposes of analysis, here, we can separate economic effects in a country from that country's political objectives, the problem of achieving political acceptability may add a *third dimension* to the task of balancing variety and interdependence.

[5]See, for example, Thomas N. Gladwin and I. Walter, *Multinationals Under Fire* (Wiley, New York, 1980); Louis Turner, *Oil Companies in the International System* (Allen and Unwin, London, 1978); and Yves Doz, *Multinational Strategic Management: Economic and Political Imperatives*, draft, 1980.
[6]Joseph L. Bower and Y. Doz, "Strategy Formulation: A Social and Political Process," in Schendel and Hofer (Eds.), *Strategic Management: A New View of Business Policy and Planning* (Little Brown, New York, 1979).

MANAGERIAL CHALLENGES IN MNC–NATIONAL GOVERNMENT RELATIONS

Clearly the goal of host governments is to affect the performance characteristics of MNC subsidiary operations in ways they desire or to use the established MNC position as a bargaining block to seek additional local benefits. From the perspective of the multinational firm whose raison d'être is based on a network of subsidiaries within the system that responds to some common strategy and shares a common base of resources, substantive government demands or requests cannot be viewed or dealt with solely within the national setting of individual subsidiaries in which they are made.

Consequently one major challenge in managing government relations in a multinational corporate network is to understand and deal with government issues that have an impact beyond the local subsidiary and affect the interests or operations of other units (these could be other subsidiaries, functional units, other areas or product divisions) within the firm. For example, a government request for greater investment in a country reduces the pool of resources available for investment elsewhere in the system. A demand for greater value-added typically translates into a demand for greater resource allocation to that country and a reduction of exports (thus profitability) of another subsidiary within the system. Similarly, a demand for greater exports requires additional resource commitment and the curtailment of exports elsewhere in the system (assuming that the global export market potential faced by the firm remains fairly constant in the short run). These issues require some measure of intraorganizational coordination and problem solving. Decisions on such issues cannot be made satisfactorily by subsidiary managers. The parochial perspective of these individuals is reinforced by the fact that they are typically responsible for, and judged as, independent profit centers (or against budget commitments) and does not depend on their contributions to the performance of the enterprise as a whole. Thus MNCs need to provide some mechanism for affecting the intraorganizational coordination and reconciling and resolving the divergent interests of the different subunits without compromising the overall interests of the company.

A second managerial challenge involves the ability to understand and deal with the impact of decisions in one country on government relations in another country or on the relations in a different activity of the company in the same country. For example, a pharmaceutical firm pays great attention to the price of a new drug in the market of first introduction, because this initial established price may serve as a benchmark for that product in other countries; or an industrial company responds favorably to a government request for local value-added for one product line because it fears that not doing so may result in loss of import licenses for other product lines. Similarly, an MNC must pay careful attention to choice of technology. Submitting to a demand for use of labor-intensive technology may affect the quality of its products and damage the brand image elsewhere.

Assessing the precedent-setting implications of an issue lies outside the purview of country managements in whose domain they may originate. Individually, the response to a single issue in a country may be seen as a constraint on the strategy of the firm's operation in that country, but where wider government ramifications can result the collective impact on the firm's worldwide operations may be far broader in magnitude. Identifying and managing these situations calls for managers with corporatewide perspective and some measure of intraorganization coordination.

Finally, a third managerial challenge arises from the fact that a multinational company frequently finds itself confronting similar government demands or pressures in various countries that seem to require similar solutions. In such cases there may be economies to be gained from organizational learning by developing the ability to transfer knowledge and experience from one decision situation to another. For example, a pharmaceutical firm facing rather similar product registration procedures in different countries could benefit by instituting standardized procedures for disseminating the product research, technical, and evaluative information developed in different parts of the system.

The managerial challenges of government issues faced by the multinational companies just discussed are of primary interest in this study because they are specific to multinational firms as a class.

It should be noted that still another set of government issues, based on the laws and regulations in any country, generally applies equally to all firms in that country—local and multinational. Countries tend to have distinct public policy climates: a plethora of laws and regulations governing the conduct of business activities such as firm registration, zoning requirements, environmental protection, pollution control, worker health and safety, industrial relations, product standards, and specifications. The multinational firm, operating in several countries, faces a set of public policy climates that may differ substantially from country to country. Hence the firm's subsidiaries in two countries may be subject to different product standards and environmental protection regulations. These differences in public policy climates drive the MNC toward custom tailoring or adaptation to local policy environments.

Provided that this set of issues does not have an international impact beyond the country in question, the management of these issues devolves on subsidiary managers. But the existence and extent of international impact is dependent on a company's strategy; for example, labor relations policy is usually left to the subsidiary. However, for a firm operating a network of interdependent plants across countries labor strife in one country may place manufacturing operations in other countries at risk. In such a situation area division management is likely to follow closely a subsidiary's handling of labor relations.

Managers of multinational subsidiaries, being more familiar with their country environments, are usually responsible for managing the firm's response to these country-specific issues and enjoy considerable latitude in doing so. Subsidiary managers usually join managers of local industry and national trade associations that are seeking to provide business feedback to governments concerning changes in regulations. In responding to the variegation of public policy climates it faces, the MNC behaves as a collection of national subsidiaries, each, in general, responding as independently and individually to its public policy climate as purely local firms would. As such this category of issues makes no special demands on an MNC and is not considered further in this study.

MULTINATIONAL ORGANIZATION STRUCTURE: THE CONTEXT FOR MANAGING GOVERNMENT ISSUES

The managerial challenges posed by government issues must be understood and managed in the context of the organization structure of the MNC.

The organization structure of an MNC is generally driven by strategic demands other than that of managing its relations with host governments. The formal structure embodies the balance that has to be struck among the product, functional, and geographic perspectives of the company's operations.

Firms with few foreign operations are content with an international division structure to oversee their foreign operations. However, as the size and importance of foreign operations increase, economic pressures to coordinate and integrate along functional dimensions also increase, particularly in the manufacturing, research, and finance functions. As the number of foreign plants grows, considerable economies of scale can be

effected by rationalizing and integrating manufacturing operations worldwide. Most companies retain central control of R&D
because the economies and pressures to do so are strong.

Multinational companies in research-intensive industries feel
the strong need to transfer specialized *product* information and
assistance from the parent company to its subsidiaries overseas.
Technical product information, manufacturing technology, and
often marketing skills are all required by foreign affiliates as increasingly sophisticated products are manufactured and sold
abroad. This technological interdependence between domestic
and foreign divisions for products tends to favor products
rather than markets as the primarily organizational dimension
of the firm, thereby allowing specialized product communication and technological assistance to flow worldwide.

Other examples of how organization structure is driven by
company strategy—not government relations—are those of
companies relying on rationalized or integrated production to
lower manufacturing costs or those with mature product lines
that serve common end-users. Such companies tend to have
area-dominated structures that permit them to coordinate product and parts flow within a self-contained region. Marketing-
intensive companies tend to have *country*-dominated area
structures because the key tasks are focused at the national
level, with little long-term advantage to be gained by global or
regional integration of operations.

In theory, a multinational matrix organization could accommodate two primary strategic perspectives at the same time by
emphasizing shared responsibility and dual reporting lines. In
practice, the maintenance of the power balance between two
"equal" perspectives is always tenuous. A clear observable fact
across multinational companies is the lack of enthusiasm for
such a complex organization. Besides, there is little evidence in
theory or practice to suggest that companies would select government relations as one of the two strategic perspectives rather
than a combination of product, function, or geography. In most

multinationals, however, the principle of unity of command still reigns.

Whatever the primary structural dimension along which the firm is organized, the organizational problem facing managers of MNCs is to resolve the various pressures created by opposing organizational demands. Technological and economic pressures argue for central coordination and integration of key functional and product strategies. Government demands tend to pull toward fragmentation of strategy and self-contained national operations responsive to local demands and decentralized responsibilities within the firm. But the managerial challenge of government issues is seldom so overwhelming that it becomes the dominant organizational dimension in an MNC, superseding other pressures; neither can these issues be ignored altogether. Clearly they have to be managed in a more or less organized fashion within the context of the firm's dominant orientation reflected in the current structure.

Multinational companies are not all equally affected by government issues. As such, the relative importance of government relations varies widely from firm to firm. Three factors suggest how important management of government relations can be to a firm: the salience of the industry, the international strategy of the company, and the spread of its international operations.

A salient industry is one in which governments have a keen and abiding interest (due to the importance of the industry as a source of the country's revenues, to its centrality in the development of the national technological or industrial base, or to the importance of its contribution to national employment or income). In salient industries, the range of interaction between the firm and the governments will be more frequent and encompassing. It will also be more likely that the firm will encounter greater constraints as a result of governmental demands.

Not all international strategies open to a multinational firm are equally vulnerable to government demands or intervention. When a firm's overseas operations are highly integrated and interdependent, government demands are more important in terms of their potential as constraints on the achievement of the firm's objectives. At the extreme a firm producing in one central location has no broader impacts to consider. It operates as a national firm in that one country. Of course, if it relies on exporting a part of this production, it still has to worry about policies of its major country markets. But, relatively, even the restrictive actions of a single government are unlikely to jeopardize its network seriously unless it relies substantially on the restricting country's market.

Thus, in general, the benefits of increased organized management and coordination of government issues will be greater (or the costs of neglect will be higher) for firms in salient industries as opposed to those in less salient and nonsalient industries. Similarly, the benefits will be higher (or costs of neglect greater) for firms pursuing integrated operations overseas in relation to those producing from one central location or those with more or less self-contained national subsidiaries.

The spread of a firm's international network also affects the constellation of costs and benefits of government-relations management. The larger a multinational network, the more opportunities a firm will have to experience a similar class of issues and to perceive its importance and, consequently, the more significant the gains from learning. The benefits to a firm from developing an ability to transfer relevant information and experience from one situation to the next are high. At the same time, however, the larger the spread, the more incumbent it is on the firm to develop an organized approach toward managing government issues, as effective informal handling of such issues becomes difficult. A large firm may wish to avoid the penalties of inconsistent responses that may ensue.

ARCHETYPICAL APPROACHES

At the outset it should be noted that management of the substantive issues in company-government relations is not analogous to management of the finance or R&D function within the multinational firm. The range and significance of issues that can, potentially, crop up is large and varied, and as such it is impossible to differentiate a government-affairs function that could oversee or manage all the issues facing a firm in this area. Rather, the process of managing company-government issues should be viewed as an activity that intimately affects the strategic, operational, and structural choices made by a firm and that involves line executives and managers across organizational hierarchies and functions as well as staff.

In seeking to develop a conceptual framework on which multinational companies could deal with the managerial challenges of government relations, the work of three major organizational theorists provides valuable concepts. Cyert and March, in their much heralded *A Behavioral Theory of the Firm*, studied organizational decisions, as choices made in terms of goals, on the basis of expectations. At the heart of their theory of business decisions are four concepts: quasi-resolution of conflict, uncertainty avoidance, problemistic search, and organizational learning.[7] A brief explanation of each concept and discussion of the implications for this research follows:

Quasi-Resolution of Conflict. An organization is made up of members having different goals. In general, there is no internal consensus within a firm at the level of operational goals. Nevertheless, organizations thrive with considerable latent goal conflict. The prevailing coalition imposes on the organization a series of independent aspiration-level constraints. Individual subunits deal with a limited set of problems and a limited set of goals. Conflict among goals is resolved by sequential attention to goals. Inconsistencies that occur are absorbed by organizational slack.

Whether such "local rationality," postulated by Cyert and March, will resolve the conflict depends, of course, on whether

[7]Richard M. Cyert and James G. March, *A Behavioral Theory of the Firm* (Prentice-Hall, Englewood, NJ, 1963).

the decisions generated by the system are consistent with one another and with the demands of the external environment. When environmental feedback is negative, however, there is a possibility that a dominant coalition may emerge and impose its views on the organization. The greater the penalties faced by the organization as a result of the feedback, the more likely this is to occur. This consensus may be codified in rules of procedures that govern specific key decision areas which are treated as exceptions to the operation of local rationality. Hence the dominant coalition (in which top management is the prime component) can force subunits to subjugate their interests for the larger interests of the whole firm (as defined by the dominant coalition). Situations are construed as standard. The rules and procedures enacted ensure performance. They make possible regular or coordinated activity. Because procedures are standardized, they do not change quickly or easily.

Uncertainty Avoidance. Uncertainty is an unavoidable feature of the environment in which organizations must live. Organizations desire to avoid uncertainty in one of two ways: they choose to solve pressing problems, thus avoiding the requirement that they anticipate events in the future, or they negotiate with the environment. The requirement that future reactions be anticipated is avoided by the imposition of plans, standard operating procedures, industry tradition, and contracts on the environment.

These two ways are quite different from each other and serve to distinguish between two of our archetypes (ad hoc versus policy) presented later.

Problemistic Search. Organizations satisfy rather than optimize. They select the first alternative that meets acceptable-level goals. The search is problem-oriented and follows simple-minded rules that look first to the neighborhood of the problem symptoms and next to the neighborhood of the current alternative.

Cyert and March, however, acknowledge the existence of bias

in search procedure. The search is biased by the special training and experience of the various parts of the organization, the interaction of hopes and expectations, and the communication patterns between subunits. This implies that instead of random or independent bias, which occurs when conflicts are resolved under local rationality, *systematic* bias in search procedure can be introduced by the consistent involvement of certain subunits on issues of a certain class as a result of their goals, training, and experience. By prescribing the composition of search units the dominance, or at least the input, of certain perspectives can be assured. By focusing attention on inputs the nature of outputs can be affected.

Organizational Learning. Behavior (characterized by the three concepts) tends to be quite stable. Being dynamic institutions, however, organizations adapt in the light of their experience. Organizational learning results in changes in goals, decision rules, and search procedures.

The concept of organizational learning provides for gradual change. Organizational priorities, perceptions, and procedures change incrementally. Changes consist typically of the marginal adaptation of existing rules and activities.

Jay Galbraith addresses the question of how conflicts may be resolved and the interests of different subunits reconciled in his book, *Designing Complex Organizations*:

> The final organization design strategy is to employ lateral forms of communication and joint decision-making processes. That is, instead of referring a problem upward in the hierarchy, the managers solve the problem at their own level, contacting and cooperating with peers in those departments affected by new information. . . . There are several forms of lateral relations. Some are simple, obvious, and inexpensive. Others are more sophisticated, costly, and require more design attention.[8]

[8]Jay Galbraith, *Designing Complex Organizations* (Addison-Wesley, Reading, MA, 1973).

These organizational mechanisms may take a range of forms. They include direct contact between managers who share a problem, temporary task forces to solve problems affecting several departments, more permanent groups or teams for constantly recurring interdepartmental problems, and new, integrating roles when leadership of lateral processes becomes a concern. These forms are listed in order of increasing cost. Organizations utilize them in proportion to the amount of task uncertainty. Thus, as task uncertainty increases, the organization will adopt these mechanisms sequentially. Higher forms are added to, not substituted for, lower forms.[9]

Drawing on these concepts and experiential knowledge, one can postulate three archetypical categories of responses, or management models, that multinationals could be expected to adopt in dealing with government issues. The three archetypes are the Ad Hoc Approach, the Policy Approach, and the Organizational Overlay Approach. Each archetype emphasizes different attributes of the concepts already discussed. These archetypes or models are presented here as distinct and parallel pure types. This does not, however, mean that a multinational firm is equally likely to adopt any one of these three approaches. Indeed, based on the attributes of each archetype, it is possible to make specific propositions about the kinds of multinational corporations whose management of government relations will reflect the primacy of those attributes.

Model 1: The Ad Hoc Approach

In the Ad Hoc Approach government issues are dealt with individually as and when they arise. Firms solve pressing government-related problems rather than developing long-term strategies or solutions. They avoid the necessity of anticipating events in the distant future by using decision-rules emphasizing short-run reaction to short-run feedback.

[9]*Ibid.*

Government issues are seen as inadequately foreseeable or as exogenous to the firm. Similarly, firms obviate the necessity of specifying a priori trade-offs or making hard choices among goals. In this way they avoid intraorganizational conflict among the interests of constituent subunits until their hands are forced. Incompatible constraints are attended to sequentially, with the organization satisfying some while simply neglecting others. How an issue is handled may depend on where the situation arises and on the perceptions, priorities, and personalities of frontline players. In the absence of policies or guidelines there is considerable leeway for front-line managers in framing the context of the problem, specifying choices, and making proposals. Thus, as a problem develops, the firm's subunits immediately involved deal with it in terms of the constraints they see as being most important. When the next problem occurs, another group of subunits deals with it in terms of a different set of constraints. Little organizational learning is accumulated. Top management concerns revolve around "how to preserve my leeway until time clarifies uncertainties."

By solving government issues after they appear ad hoc companies afford themselves considerable flexibility of response. At the same time, however, by not anticipating government demands firms risk being overwhelmed by them; by not emphasizing consistency of response they run the risk of setting harmful precedents from one situation to the next.

In seeking to identify those companies that adopt the Ad Hoc Approach to their dealings with host governments, one can readily point to those with relatively few operations or those that are relative newcomers to the international scene. More generally, companies pursuing the Ad Hoc Approach are likely to be those for which the cost of potential mismanagement or neglect of government issues is less than the cost of a more anticipatory or coordinated approach to deal with them.

Model 2: The Policy Approach

The Policy Approach takes an opposite position from the Ad Hoc Approach. Rather than wait for governments to act, a firm seeks to address preemptively the major areas of government concern in a set of centrally developed, explicitly enunciated policies and guidelines. The policy framework specifies at the outset the tradeoffs a company is willing to make or accept. These policies are then offered—or, more accurately, imposed on—host governments as the unequivocal terms and conditions that govern the entry and operations of the company in their country. By imposing these self-generated, uncertainty-absorbing contracts on host governments policy-oriented companies clearly integrate their government-relations strategies into their overall corporate strategies.

The Policy Approach obviates the need to take into account future reactions of governments. It seeks to regularize the reactions of governments with whom they deal. By offering their policies as conventional practice everywhere companies seek to establish a uniform status quo. It diminishes the need for frequent negotiations with various governments over similar issues requiring case-by-case decisions.

Top-management actions are governed by this concern: "how to ensure consistent and systematic response across issue-areas, such that government issues do not compromise our operations." Top management lays great stress at the outset on central coordination recognizing that important problems overlap jurisdictions of several subunits. The existence of such a framework ensures consistent application of solutions by country or regional subunits confronted with decision-situations that fall in these areas. The search process is routinized and choice of action predetermined. Irrespective of where the issue originates within the regular structure of the firm, by spelling out its policies the firm incorporates government-relations responsibilities into the regular structure of the firm. Thus only cases that cannot be adequately dealt with within the existing policy parameters are forced upward for top-management consideration.

The inherent proactive posture suggests the risk of locking the firm into explicit policies if it does not provide for a mechanism by which these policies can be changed. For change to occur significant pressures must exist.

Companies pursuing this approach are likely to be those that stand to gain significant benefits from an anticipatory, centrally developed, and imposed Policy Approach toward government issues. To maintain this approach a firm must have considerable bargaining power to impose its will and sustain the stability of its policies.

Model 3: The Organizational Overlay Approach

This approach is characterized by the existence of specialized government-affairs staffs and the use of one or more lateral coordination mechanisms, such as temporary task forces, project teams, and working groups, and includes permanent teams or formal coordinating managerial roles—all of which share the primary objective of coordinating and managing government issues. Issue responses are not preemptively determined, but organizational mechanisms do exist to ensure the required shifts in decision-locus to include the perspectives of the affected (or appropriate) subunits within the firm or to capture and transfer information and experience from one situation to the next.

The governing assumption of companies in this approach is that, whereas the broad government issue-areas can be anticipated, the specific manner in which the issue will manifest itself cannot be prescribed. An inordinate amount of uncertainty pervades the details surrounding circumstances of issue manifestation; and these details or circumstances are important in assessing the stakes and attendant risks. In other words, problems are not deemed to be standard. Thus response-development has to await the issue. What distinguishes this approach from the ad hoc however, is that companies here recognize the necessity that something must be done to manage government issues. Top management stresses the process of making decisions on various classes of issues and provides the requisite mechanism to support the process. The organization mechanisms thus developed may serve as gatherers of information and monitors of government issues in addition to affecting actual management of issues once they have arisen. In the latter case these units bear the responsibility of carefully assessing the crucial consequences of whatever is done.

Some of these organizational units are specified at the outset; others are real-time decisions necessitated by the highly atypical circumstances of a case. In either case top management has the opportunity to determine consciously the composition of these units, be they temporary or permanent. By its selection of managers with different perspectives and different training management ensures the requisite bias in problem definition, choice of alternatives, and the manner in which proposals are pushed. The quality of decisions depends on the form and composition of mechanisms provided for response formation and resolution of conflict.

This approach in its pure form lies somewhere between the Ad Hoc Approach and the Policy Approach. Firms in this category do not have the bargaining power to impose their policies on government issues but stand to benefit sufficiently from a coordinated and organized approach to government issues.

The three models are obviously not exclusive alternatives. Indeed, the paradigms highlight the partial emphasis of each framework—what each magnifies and what it leaves out. Each concentrates on certain attributes, relegating others to a ceteris paribus clause. Along one dimension they represent different patterns of activity: purposive action toward strategic objectives (the Policy Approach), institutionalized behavior toward different organizational goals (the Organizational Overlay Approach), or the nondirective approach toward resolution of competing goals (the Ad Hoc Approach).

Along another dimension they represent different levels of aggregation. The policy model sees the firm as a unitary actor with the different subunits subjugating their differing perspectives and interests and responding to a single common framework. The other two models provide much greater emphasis on the interplay of organizational politics, as subunits with different goals compete to protect their interests.

These paradigms and propositions, however, are presented as a conceptual framework to provide a useful guide to the more complex realities of firm behavior in the real world.

RESEARCH METHODOLOGY

In attempting to define a specific research methodology for the questions posed in this study, it was anticipated—and quickly substantiated—that a direct inquiry concerning a firm's government-relations strategy or its "organization for managing government relations" was a nonstarter. To begin with, the term "government-relations management" means different things to different people. For some managers a study in this area conjured up images of investigative journalism into international corruption scandals; others saw government-relations management as an extension of the public-relations function of the firm; and not a few executives were extremely sensitive in discussing the issues involved in government relations. To them the area represented a potential mine field in which anything said could violate important confidences or reveal deep embarrassments.

The underlying problem, of course, was that it was impossible to differentiate a specific government-relations function because of the wide range of issues that fall within its rubric. In reality, the bulk of government-related issues is dispersed through the various functional, product, and area hierarchies. As such, these issues affect ongoing strategic and operational decisions of the firm. Few executives, therefore, had any more than the most general outline or description of the management of government relations that characterized their own firm's activities in the international arena.

Thus it was decided that rather than direct inquiry the best approach would be to focus on a few important government-related issues or events within the recent memory or experience of its senior executives. Further, to understand how different firms might deal with a common set of issues and to ensure an adequate profile of a firm's government-relations approach across a variety of issues, the researcher posed common hypothetical scenarios in different issue areas to all firms. Quite frequently these scenarios prompted managers to recall parallel real-life experiences. The process by which the company formulated its response and dealt with the government was then explored in some depth with the managers and executives involved. Through a compendium of issues generated by these approaches, supported by a general line of questioning, a picture of the government-relations strategy and structure was gradually developed.

The primary sample of companies from which the data for this research were drawn represents a broad range of industries—computers, telecommunications, automobiles, pharmaceuticals, agricultural and construction equipment, office equipment, diesel engines, and petroleum. The sample size was 13 companies, six of which were oil producers. Marketing-oriented companies were deliberately excluded because they tend to pursue strong, locally oriented strategies that often make them difficult to distinguish from domestic firms.

All in all, some 180 interviews were gathered and analyzed. Because the perspective sought involved both strategic and operational dimensions, interviews were held with managers at different levels and with different perspectives. In most firms the range of interviewees included senior corporate, product, and/or division executives and major functional and country managers.

REAL-WORLD MODES

In their actual behavior companies manifest some attributes from each of the three archetypes. As is common in this kind of research, the desired balance between detail and generalization is always problematic: at one extreme it can be argued that each company follows its own unique approach, based on its own particular requirements and the peculiarities of the international environment in which it operates. The aim of this study, however, is to define and isolate the common elements, particularly with regard to the strategy process, and structure of government-relations management across companies. In so doing much rests on the researcher's judgment.

The firms that I observed seemed to fall into three broad categories: the *Diffuse Mode*, which most closely parallels the Ad Hoc Archetype; the *Assertive Mode*, which draws prominently from the Policy and Organizational Overlay Archetypes; and the *Structured Mode*, which most closely resembles the Organizational Overlay Archetype. The use of different labels for real-world modes as opposed to those used for archetypes is motivated by a desire to capture the complexities of actual firm behavior from the paradigms of the archetypes. Companies were classified according to the dominant strain of attributes they exhibited.

The four Assertive Mode companies are distinguished by their conscious government-relations strategy of seeking a negotiated environment. This strategy encompasses two broad approaches. One company resembles the policy archetype and has an explicit policy framework that it imposes on governments. Others engage in negotiations with governments to specify the broad contours of the future environment in which they would be operating, but even the latter have internal guidelines that specify acceptable trade-offs. In general, the companies in this mode share an anticipatory approach toward management of government issues.

The government-relations processes include an array of organizational mechanisms that tend to vary systematically according to the nature of the issue. This is true for both internal development of corporate response and the process of company-government interface. Responsibility for individual issues devolves on line managers and functional staffs in the regular structure of the firm. Like the Organizational Overlay Archetype, these companies make extensive use of extrastructural mechanisms for affecting internal coordination.

Firms in the Assertive Mode operate in industries considered salient by governments. With one exception they pursued a strategy of integrated operations overseas.

Diffuse Mode companies perceive government issues as being exogenous to their concerns, and their government-relations strategy can best be described as "deal with governments only when you must." No explicit policies are articulated on government issues and no implicit policies can be discerned. Like the Ad Hoc Archetype, they deal with government issues on a case-by-case basis. In these firms major issues of government relations were left to lower level managers. The designation of who would handle a particular issue was ad hoc and generally depended a great deal on who seized the initiative. Few limits were placed on the freedom of the manager to respond in ways that he or she deemed appropriate to the demands of the host government. The general stance was typically a reactive one, for management waited for issues to form and then dealt with them without planned procedures or responses.

The internal processes for dealing with individual issues are varied: issues within a class may be dealt with differently depending on the front-line managers involved. Diffuse companies evidence a distinct lack of structural mechanisms for dealing with government issues. Nor is there any attempt to explicitly or implicitly cultivate an awareness for managing government relations within the existing organization structure.

The two firms in this mode displayed the hypothesized characteristics of firms pursuing an Ad Hoc Approach. They operate in nonsalient industries. One company is in the process of cautiously developing its international operations; the other is a domestically oriented international company rather than a real multinational.

The six organizations (all oil companies) in the Structured Mode live in a constantly negotiated environment in which all issues are considered negotiable. This is due to the dominance of government power over their activities. Company bargaining power is highly issue- and situation-specific. As such, management of government issues is a central feature of life in the Structured Mode.

Government-relations activities permeate the organizations. The necessity for continual negotiations with governments has resulted in the establishment of well defined processes and structures and the development of a "government negotiations" function within the organizational structure of these companies. Like the Organization Overlay Archetype, in which the broad issue areas can be foreseen, response formulation depends greatly on the specific circumstances at hand. As such, anticipatory policies are not developed. Like their archetype counterparts, they feature the requisite organizational mechanisms for bringing to bear the relevant expertise on different issue areas.

Firms in the Structured Mode operate in highly salient industries. The integrated nature of their worldwide operations tends to accentuate their vulnerability. Because they possess a large spread, these companies take into account the global impact of any response decision.

2
The Assertive Mode

ASSERTIVE MODE DEFINED

The Assertive Mode of government-relations management describes a range of multinational companies whose approach to the management of overseas operations reflects a keen sensitivity to government interests and concerns born out of an active awareness of the power of national regulations and government market power over company affairs. For companies in this mode the management of government relations is perceived as an integral part of all strategic and operational decision making.

Two fundamental characteristics distinguish the Assertive Mode from other modes in this study: (1) an emphasis on proactive, anticipatory policies and government-relations strategies and (2) the ability to articulate and secure favorable outcomes across a wide range of issues in the company–government negotiations process.

The primary focus of Assertive company strategies is the establishment of a "negotiated environment" with the host country government. By "negotiated environment" we are referring to a reconciliation process that features some understanding be-

27

tween the company and government in which company needs
and government demands are sought to be translated into long-
term agreements or concordats, with the responsibilities and
obligations of both parties specified, articulated, and enacted.
Through the reconciliation of government concerns or demands
with company needs, Assertive managers seek to minimize uncertainty and to create a reasonably stable operating environment in which ongoing or surprise government intervention in
the company's business decisions are kept to a minimum. This
contrasts sharply with Diffuse Mode strategies in which companies view government issues as external to regular corporate interests and deal with them only when required to do so.

While seeking to create a reasonably certain long-term environment, Assertive managers invariably circumscribe their freedom of action in the near-term, thus reducing their short-term
flexibility. This "penalty" is not generally felt by companies in
the Diffuse Mode, whose passive ad hoc style of government-
relations management leaves considerable room for opportun-
ism; nor is it generally a concern of Structured companies for
whom all issues of government concern are subject to continual
negotiations in a highly structured environment.

The companies in the Assertive Mode can also be described
as displaying a combination of the characteristics of the three
"pure-type" approaches to government-relations management
postulated in Chapter One: particularly the Policy Approach
and the Organizational Overlay Approach. In the policy-pure
type it will be recalled that companies are able to impose their
own centrally developed policies on host governments, whereas
in the Organizational Overlay Approach companies with generally weaker bargaining strength tend to develop organizational
structures and mechanisms to cope with a whole range of government issues. Companies in the Assertive Mode generally fall
somewhere between the two, relying on well defined company
policies and guidelines but submitting to the necessity for inter-
active bargaining on a wide range of issues. The specific balance between the two approaches is primarily determined by

the relative bargaining power of each party as well as on the nature and importance of the issue or issues at hand.

The specific organizational processes that facilitate the management of government relations in Assertive companies tend to be relatively defined and explicit in terms of the internal corporate response to government issues and the external management of company–government relations. These processes generally involve a wide array of organizational mechanisms and procedures, which, again, vary according to the particular issue involved. Finally, the organizational structure and administrative systems of the Assertive companies reflect to some degree a conscious and deliberate attempt to attend to and facilitate the management of government relations. Though the management of individual issues generally falls on line and functional staffs, companies make regular use of extrastructural mechanisms for affecting internal coordination and some have well defined procedures for conflict resolution and specialized government affairs staffs as well. Thus Assertive companies have developed the capacity and the "tools" to articulate and implement specific government-related objectives and manage their relations with the host governments of the countries in which they operate.

The preceding description permits inclusion of companies in the Assertive Mode that represent a wide range of organization types and display a variety of strategic approaches to international operations. For example, IBM and ITT pursue diametrically opposed international strategies (integrated versus country-oriented) and possess vastly different organizational structures. At the same time, however, they clearly pursue an activist, anticipatory approach to their management of government relations.

On the basis of these criteria, four companies in this study fell into the Assertive Mode: International Business Machines (IBM) in the computer industry, Ford Motor Company (Ford) in the automotive industry, Eli Lilly and Co. (Lilly) in the health-care field, and International Telephone and Telegraph Corporation (ITT) in telecommunications. Although firms like Ford, Lilly, and ITT operate diversified businesses, this study examined their management of government relations in their dominant business sector.

To understand why such a diverse group of companies would choose to be Assertive managers of government relations it is important to note the substantial similarities among them. First, all four companies operate in industries that are regarded as highly salient by host governments and are subject to considerable scrutiny and regulatory controls. Second, with the notable exception of ITT, all pursue integrated strategies in their management of international operations, manufacturing, and R&D. Finally, all four are multinationals in the fullest sense of the word: all conduct manufacturing activities in more than a dozen countries and maintain marketing and service operations in many more. Their extensive international networks testify to their substantial overseas experience and all are considered major competitors in the markets in which they operate.

Companies adopt an assertive approach toward management of government relations when the cost of ignoring government issues or dealing with them individually as they appear becomes greater than the cost of organizing to deal with them in a consistent and coordinated manner. The three company characteristics that define these costs and benefits are the extent of government involvement in—or active concern with—the industrial sector in which the firms operate, the vulnerability of their international strategies, and the breadth of their international operations.

CHARACTERISTICS OF COMPANIES: CHALLENGES IN GOVERNMENT-RELATIONS MANAGEMENT

Each of the three characteristics that directly influence the importance of government-relations management to a firm—the salience of the industry to host governments, the specific company strategies pursued, and the breadth of company operations—has a different implication for the firm in terms of necessitating company attention to host government concerns.

Influence of Industry Salience

Computers, automobiles, health care, and telecommunications are all considered by governments to be important industries within a national economy. Typically, these industries are among the largest industrial sectors in a country and all contribute significantly to the national income. Because of the economic requirement of scale economies in manufacturing and R&D, firms in these industries are dominated by a few large actors—primarily large multinational corporations. It is therefore not surprising that all four companies in our sample attract considerable national attention and must deal with a wide range of government demands and requests. Though a detailed account of the international industry structures and the role of government involvement is outside the scope of this present study, it is appropriate to examine briefly the importance of these industries to the national economies in which they operate.

The computer or data processing industry epitomizes the technological revolution in microelectronics that has been occurring over the last two decades. It is generally considered to be the leading high-technology industry and is increasingly viewed as fundamental to a country's national industrial base. According to one French government commission, the importance of the computer industry to the national economy is demonstrated in three basic areas:

1. It employs an increasingly large number of highly skilled, well trained people in R&D, manufacturing, and service.

2. Its products serve as basic tools in all industries for R&D, manufacturing, and management (including industries vital to national defense).

3. The way in which a country succeeds in developing and mastering data processing techniques will increasingly become a measure of its technological independence.[1]

In seeking to "redeploy" their industrial bases toward the high-growth, high-technology "industries of the future," many governments have launched enthusiastically into the computer business under the sponsorship of "national champions" which benefit from a wide range of government purchasing preference policies, grants, and subsidies.[2] The results, however, have been distinctly mediocre.[3] One explanation points to the global nature of the computer industry. IBM, for example, will argue that its own success at establishing and maintaining a dominant presence in the field is due as much to its exploitation of high-scale economies and worldwide marketing strategies as it is to its technological leadership. National champions, on the other hand, hamstrung by the national limits of government policy frameworks, have yet to come close to IBM's lead. Nevertheless, most governments remain highly sensitive to the operations of foreign computer companies in their countries and in some cases have succeeded in negotiating joint ventures as one method of promoting national interests in this area.[4]

The automobile industry has often been described as the

[1]Yves Doz, *Multinational Strategic Management: Economic and Political Imperatives*, draft, 1980.
[2]G. Nakae, "Market Strategies in the Computer Industry," and the EEC Commission's "Report Concerning the Development of the Data Processing Sector in the Community in Relation to the World's Situation," *EEC-COM Report No. 76-524*, Brussels, 1976.
[3]P. Gadonneix, *The Plan Calcul* (unpublished doctoral dissertation), Harvard Graduate School of Business Administration, Boston, MA., 1975.
[4]The Honeywell-CII joint venture is a classic case.

"most important manufacturing industry in the world."[5] In the major developed nations of North America, Western Europe, and Japan autos account for 7 to 10% of all manufacturing output, 20% of all retail sales, and 5 to 8% of total manufacturing employment. With substantial purchases in the iron, steel, machine tools, rubber, copper, aluminum, glass, plastics, electronics and petroleum industries, its multiplier effects rebound to nearly every corner of the national economy. Moreover, in many countries its international receipts account for a significant share of the national balance of payments: for example, in 1980 Japan's surplus auto trade with the United States alone amounted to $12 billion—almost the entire difference between the trade balances of the two countries. At the same time reduced car exports from Europe threatened to compromise severely the trade balances of Germany, Italy, and France. In the countries of the developing world the size, scale, and multiplier effects of the auto industry have similar impacts on national economies.

The auto industry has had a long history of government involvement, though industrial policies directed toward automobile companies have evolved considerably over the years.[6] During the last decade the nature of government intervention in the field has been largely shaped by the openness of the particular trade policies it pursues. In Western Europe, for example, where member countries of the EEC generally adopt liberal free-trade policies, governments promote national auto industries through a combination of direct assistance, grants and subsi-

[5]Mira Wilkins, "Multinational Automobile Enterprises and Regulation: An Historical Overview," in *Government, Technology and the Automobile Industry*, William Abernathy and D. Ginsburg (Eds.) (McGraw-Hill, New York, 1980).
[6]See note on the Auto Sector Policies of France, Germany, and Japan, draft, Harvard Business School, Boston, MA. 1981. For historical surveys of European government policies toward the automobile industry see Louis T. Wells, Jr., "Automobiles," in *Big Business and the State*, R. Vernon (Ed.) (Harvard University Press, Cambridge, 1974); see also Mira Wilkins, *op. cit.*

dies, regional development incentives, and loan guarantees. In developing countries, such as Brazil, Mexico, Nigeria, and Korea, which pursue more protectionist norms, investment by foreign auto manufacturers is generally controlled by a balance of incentives and restrictions, offering access to their fast-growing markets and low factor costs in exchange for adherence to tight investment policies such as local value-added requirements, import restrictions, and export quotas.

The health-care industry—and the ethical-drugs and hospital-supplies subsectors, in particular—is one of the most highly regulated industries in the world.[7] Most advanced countries have developed extensive regulatory policies and structures that tightly control the introduction of new drugs into the market. These policies in general not only require the submission of clinical tests on safety and efficacy but also the adherence to a plethora of rules on product performance, manufacturing processes, and product pricing.

Since the late 1960s, when the Colombian government decided to enforce a $3.3 million price reduction on a national drug import bill of $15 million, the issue of drug "transfer pricing" has become an increasing preoccupation of national regulatory agencies. In the United Kingdom, for example, government concern with price controls has taken the form of a "Voluntary Price Regulation Scheme" (VPRS), which involves a complicated drug-pricing formula based on sales, expense, and investment data. In the late 1970s the government tightened the "voluntary" aspect of this policy and in one highly published case cut and froze reimbursements to Hoffmann-LaRoche for products sold to the National Health Services when the company refused to disclose sufficient cost and profit information.[8] Numerous other countries have also instituted complex pricing formulas and rules, particularly in Europe, where government-

[7]J.E. Schnee, "International Shifts in Innovational Activity: The Case of Pharmaceuticals," Columbia Journal of World Business, Spring 1978.
[8]R. Weerasinghe and T. Leonhard, F. Hoffman-LaRoche & Co., A.G., ICCH Case 9-376-055, 1975.

sponsored health services are often the major purchasers of drug products. The United States has also become more active in this area with the recent enactment of the FDA's new "Maximum Allowance Cost" scheme (MAC), which is designed to limit Medicare and Medicaid reimbursements to the lowest priced "equivalent product." It should be noted here that one of the primary motivations behind these policies in recent years has been the increasingly severe effects of inflation on hospital costs and medical care and the consequent threats to the "survivability" of national health care policies. One of the primary effects of this increased government regulation, however, has been to discourage drug companies from further investments in local manufacturing and R&D activities (the latter is especially significant in the drug business, often accounting for 8 to 9% of sales). To be sure, the industry trend in recent years has been toward a rationalization of international manufacturing, marketing, and R&D at the expense of local operations in order to maintain margins by cost control.

The telecommunications equipment industry is also characterized by extensive government regulation and control over its markets, where state-owned post, telephone, and telegraph companies (PTTs) and government agencies are by far the major customers. One study estimated that government shares of the telecommunications markets in Western Europe ranged from 55% in Germany to 70% in France[9]; in developing countries it frequently approaches 100%.

In this connection the growth and development of state-owned PTTs provide a classic case study of the phenomenon of "state-owned enterprises" and the increasing influence of political authority in the process of economic development.[10] Some studies have noted the extensive role of these state-owned en-

[9]N. Jequier, *Les Telecommunications et L'Europe*, Centre d'Etudes Industrielles, Geneva, 1976; see also Y. Doz, *op. cit.*
[10]For a detailed discussion of links between government bureaucracy and the PTT in France, see J.P. Anastassopoulos, *The Strategic Autonomy of Government-Controlled Enterprises* (unpublished doctoral dissertation),

terprises as channels for the implementation of various national objectives, such as the protection of employment, trade balances, and local R&D promotion. In the case of the telecommunications industry the growth of state-owned PTTs has led to the development of a worldwide fragmentation of communications networks into separate and protected national markets. At the same time government relations with private equipment suppliers in the telecommunications industry have become highly specific. For example, PTTs are frequently in a position to specify the technological requirements of individual equipment orders and generally give priority to reliability and efficiency over cost. This has also led to a situation of close government-industry relations and the gradual consolidation of firms in the area to a few trusted equipment suppliers. In fact, one study estimated that fully 75% of the international switching market was restricted to existing domestic or MNC subsidiaries.[11] At the same time PTTs have often played a leading role in cooperative R&D efforts with private industry, including foreign subsidiaries. The British Post Office, for example, played a key role in the development of "System X"—the all-electronic exchange system—a $300 million project that involved several British telecommunications equipment manufacturers, including a subsidiary of ITT.[12]

This government control over equipment manufacturers is often even more direct, involving the use of policies such as preferential access to credit, allocation of R&D contracts, and ownership constraints (particularly in the developing countries). A clear example of this more direct government influence in the telecommunications market lies in the process by which large export contracts are negotiated and awarded. Because of the

Columbia University, 1973; see also Y. Doz, *Government Control and Multinational Strategic Management*, Praeger, New York, 1979.
[11]Arthur D. Little study quoted in Y. Doz, *Government Control and Multinational Strategic Management*, draft, 1980.
[12]*Financial Times*, September 18, 1979.

high-technology, high-capital-intensive nature of the industry, such contracts are frequently negotiated within the context of bilateral trade agreements between importing and exporting countries and are often contingent on the provision of extensive government-guaranteed export credits and subsidies. Thus private firms that bid for these contracts have little choice but to comply with government requirements on product adaptation, local content, employment, trade balances, and so on.

This brief review underlines the great importance with which these four industries—computers, automobiles, drugs, and telecommunications—are regarded by host governments and illustrates the widespread nature of government influence and control. It should be clear, however, that the ability of governments to influence the activities of foreign companies in these areas varies considerably between industries. Yves Doz and other researchers[13] have pointed out that government bargaining power vis-à-vis MNC is primarily dependent on the balance between political and economic imperatives within the industry itself. For example, government bargaining power is greater in the telecommunications and health-care industries, where, in addition to their regulatory roles, most governments wield direct marketing power as customers, than it is in the computer and automobile industries; in the latter, the lack of substantial government buyer power provides greater degrees of freedom for multinational companies to heed economic drives such as scale economies which necessitate more integrated production strategies. Thus the difference between political and economic bargaining power is also reflected in the extent to which governments are formally organized to deal with these industries. For example, in the telecommunications industry national PTTs deal frequently and directly with private suppliers; simi-

---

[13]See the cited work of Y. Doz; see also Y. Doz and C.K. Prahalad, *Facing Host Government Restrictions to Multinational Companies Strategic Freedom*, draft, May 1979.

larly, in the health-care industry foreign subsidiaries are faced with specialized national regulatory agencies, which include health ministries, national health services and price control boards. On the other hand, governments are seldom specifically organized to deal with MNCs in the computer and automobile industries. National policies are more often expressed by various functional ministries, such as Finance, Industries, Trade, and Science, whose relative influence varies considerably over time and between countries.

Despite these differences, the salience of these industries ensures that MNCs such as IBM, Ford, Lilly, and ITT will face frequent government demands on a broad range of strategic and operating issues. The challenge to these companies is great: each issue area described has a direct impact beyond the specific national environment on the operations of other subsidiaries or subunits within the company. Moreover, the continuous nature of government interest in these areas makes national priorities difficult to ignore: piecemeal or ad hoc responses may often result in decisions that are neither consistent nor complete and generally involve a considerable waste of managerial time and resources.

In light of the importance of government issues in these industries, it is not surprising that all four companies have adopted an Assertive government-relations strategy with a clear focus on a "negotiated environment" that promotes well developed policy frameworks specifically addressed to the individual issues of company and government concern. The benefits of this anticipatory and coordinated approach to government relations are further enhanced by the nature of the individual strategies pursued by these companies.

Influence of Company Strategy

The more integrated and interdependent a company's overseas subsidiaries, the more vulnerable its overall operations are to government demands or requests. However, even when corporate strategy is more country-oriented and responsive to national interests, the challenges posed by government demands are no less formidable—though substantively different. In the latter case the major challenge is not vulnerability but rather inconsistency and lack of coordination between subsidiaries.

Three of the four Assertive companies in our sample can be characterized as pursuing an "integrated" strategy in their international operations. Briefly, this involves the establishment of an international manufacturing network that relies on the specialization of products across national borders. Rather than producing complete product lines for each national market, subsidiaries in an integrated network generally concentrate on only one part of the firm's product range and, in turn, import and distribute product lines from other subunits. The primary rationale behind this approach to global operations is twofold: (1) to achieve economies of scale and (2) to exploit differences in factor costs between different markets. IBM, Ford, and Lilly pursued this general approach.

IBM's integration strategy was primarily regional in focus, with two of its groups, the United States and Europe-Middle East-Africa (EMEA), representing fully integrated, self-contained product networks. The third group created in 1974— the Americas-Far East Division—was gradually moving in that direction.[14] An important exception to this regional emphasis, however, was the centralization of control over R&D location and investment at company headquarters in Armonk, New York. At the same time the company allowed many marketing functions to remain at the national level.

Product development at Ford has also become increasingly

[14]Recently the IBM Americas/Far East Corporation was divided into two groups: the IBM Asia/Pacific Group, with headquarters in Tokyo, and the Americas Group (handling Canada and Latin America), which continues to be headquartered in North Tarrytown.

global in nature, particularly with the advent of the "world car" concept. Of all its regional divisions, Ford of Europe comes closest to this description with its highly integrated network of 20 plants across seven countries. The opposite is true, however, in its Latin American Operations, where the predominance of protectionist trade policies has led to the fragmentation of company operations into separate national markets. This same protectionism operates between regions as well, and it is significant that cross shipments of finished cars among the three areas of the International Automotive Operations is still minimal.[15]

Like IBM, Eli Lilly also retains centralized control over the key functions of R&D and product development, with most of its high-technology, capital-intensive manufacturing units located in the United States and Great Britain. However, the company also maintains a global network of 13 dosage formulation and finishing plants and markets its products in more than 130 countries.

Because of the overwhelming dominance of government customers in the telecommunications market, ITT has developed a country-oriented approach to its international operations. Briefly, this means that an ITT subsidiary typically manufactures a complete range of products for its national market, engaging only minimally in trade with other company subsidiaries. Country subsidiaries are thus relatively independent profit centers and their managers are given primary responsibility for government-relations management. However, while greatly facilitating company response to government issues, this country-oriented approach is not without its challenges: the emphasis on self-sufficient national subsidiaries can easily give rise to costly duplications in R&D efforts or harmful export competition between subsidiaries that produce the same kinds of equip-

[15]The three areas are European Automotive Operations (Ford of Europe), Latin American Automotive Operations, and Asia-Pacific Automotive. The fourth area—North American Automotive Operations—is not part of IAO.

ment. At the same time each country manager can, in the interests of his own national priorities, commit the company as a whole to investment decisions having major resource allocation implications for the entire corporation. These types of problem necessitate the creation of formal and informal companywide structures and processes aimed at intersubsidiary coordination and conflict resolution.

While allowing greater economies of scale and lower factor costs between markets, the adoption of an integrated approach to worldwide operations also greatly increases the vulnerability of the company to government demands. Given the necessity of operational divisions and close links between subsidiaries, each government request for more local value-added, greater export volume, and more R&D often necessitates compensatory adjustments throughout the company network. Moreover, the number of adjustments involved often makes for long and costly lead times between government demands and company response. Thus it is extremely important for integrated companies to take an anticipatory approach to government issues.

A company's overall corporate strategy is the force behind its management structure. As pointed out in Chapter One, it is primarily within this management structure that government issues are defined and resolved. Again, the emphasis of both IBM and Ford on a worldwide integration strategy has led to the formation of strong regional subdivisions organized around the basic functional lines of product development, manufacturing, and marketing. All of Ford's regional divisions operate as separate entities with an entire range of functional and line units, whereas IBM's regional structure reserves R&D for headquarters and delegates marketing responsibility to country managers. Eli Lilly's emphasis on an integrated approach to foreign operations has resulted in the division of its International Group into three area suborganizations, each responsible for all operations in their regions. The centralization of key functions, however, is even more pronounced in Lilly, with product planning and pricing—in addition to R&D—in the hands of functional staff at corporate and international division headquarters in the United States.

ITT's formal structure differs considerably from the other three in its emphasis on the autonomy of country management, though it retains a formal Telecommunications Product Group based in New York. The corporation also has a European Regional Office in Brussels. However, unlike IBM, Ford, or Eli Lilly, it has basically no functional authority and is comprised largely of administrative and control staffs.

Influence of Spread of International Operations

The extensive spread of operations of a large MNC frequently leads to a situation in which it faces similar government pressures or demands in different countries. This situation has both potential benefits and potential costs for the company, depending on how it chooses to address them: the potential benefit, of course, is derived from the possibility of applying similar solutions to similar problems across countries, thus providing the company with an opportunity to benefit from economies of learning and experience transfer. Exploiting this opportunity ensures consistency in decisions across countries and regions and considerably lessens the managerial resources devoted to those issues, especially in the form of top-management attention. On the other hand, the existence of similar problems across the corporate network contains a serious potential cost in terms of possibilities for undesirable precedent setting and inconsistent responses. In a worldwide integrated network this failure to respond systematically to similar problems can have global repercussions.

Multinational companies such as IBM, Ford, Eli Lilly, and ITT, with widespread international operations, seek to exploit the economies from organizational learning and to develop the ability to transfer knowledge and experience from one situation to another. They do this primarily by developing policies on major international issues that are applicable systemwide. This ensures consistency in decisions across countries or regions and reduces the managerial resources devoted to any individual case. Only those that cannot be resolved within the policy framework are brought to the attention of senior management. These companies also seek to enhance intraorganizational interchange of knowledge and experience on government issues between subsidiaries and regions via periodic corporatewide meetings of line executives and specialized international staff.

Summary

From the foregoing analysis it can be seen that large MNCs choose to adopt an assertive approach to government-relations management primarily in response to the level of government involvement in their industries. Firms in salient industries are required to respond to a broad and complex range of government issues—all of which can and do have substantial impact on their overseas operations. For globally integrated companies such as IBM, which have systemwide vulnerabilities to outside government pressure or demands, an assertive approach to government relations becomes an operating necessity; however, for more country-oriented firms such as ITT the assertive posture is a reflection of extensive government involvement and the adoption of a country-tailored strategy is driven by the need to be nationally responsive at a fundamental level. Also, in a global village connected by almost instantaneous communications and the free flow of information multinational corporations need to coordinate responses to the similar issues they face across national borders.

These factors have forced many firms to adopt a conscious

and deliberate government-relations strategy of seeking a negotiated environment and developing relatively institutionalized
processes for dealing with government issues.

GOVERNMENT-RELATIONS STRATEGY

The strategic focus of companies in the Assertive Mode is the
establishment of a negotiated environment with host governments. By "negotiated environment" we are referring to the effort to create a reasonably certain world in which clear obligations and responsibilities are established at the outset and
generally adhered to throughout the period of any agreement or
understanding. To achieve this environment company managers must be concerned not only with government demands on
them but also with the impact of their own decisions on the local economy. Thus Assertive strategies are clearly anticipatory.

For the firm the effort to delineate the rules of the game involves a careful assessment of the nature and extent of the
trade-offs it can make (or is willing to live with) in the consideration of host-government concerns. In return for these commitments to national objectives the firm then seeks to safeguard
its own freedom and flexibility in areas it deems crucial to
company strategy. The primary desire of these companies is to
minimize uncertainty and to avoid the cost of incremental adjustments to government demands.

The particular outline of this negotiated environment varies
considerably from company to company and across issue areas,
depending on the relative strengths and weaknesses of the negotiating partners and the relative importance of the issue at
hand. For example, the negotiations process does not have to be
a face-to-face arrangement; in some cases company-government
understandings are entirely implicit and require little or no direct bargaining. In other cases the nature of issues at hand
might dictate the necessity for ongoing, highly structured nego-

tiations, with bargaining patterns and expectations clearly delineated on either side. Finally, the negotiations process can reflect a whole range of particular time frames—from the very short, stop-gap measures to the establishment of elaborate contracts that detail obligations and responsibilities stretching out over ten years or more.

Within the sample of companies in the Assertive Mode IBM was the only one that deliberately sought to avoid the necessity for face-to-face bargaining with host-country officials by offering its own guarantees and centrally developed policies in lieu of any directly negotiated agreements. This *implicit* negotiations process was, of course, a direct reflection of the substantial bargaining power IBM derived from its technological and market leadership. For most companies, however, *explicit* negotiations were common, often mandatory, covering an increasingly wide range of issues. It was within the explicit bargaining process that the widest variations in strategy and technique were observable. For example, Ford's strategic emphasis in arranging a negotiated environment centered on the initial entry or investment stage when company bargaining strength vis-à-vis potential country proposals was at its highest. The specific objective of the company's bargaining process was the establishment of a comprehensive, long-term agreement that would safeguard the future operating environment of its large-scale investments for many years. This same emphasis on long-term agreements was also evidenced in situations of specific government policy developments such as the changes in Mexican and Brazilian automotive policies in the mid-1970s. On the other hand, the strategic emphasis of Eli Lilly's negotiated environment was sharply circumscribed by government requirements on new drug pricing and registration procedures. Thus, although its strategic emphasis might be long-term, it was forced to subject certain key elements of company operations to short-term piecemeal periodic negotiations with host health agencies. ITT is also forced to engage in short-term and on-going negotiations, but, unlike Eli Lilly, the scope of the bargaining process is much more comprehensive, reflecting the greater dominance of governmental control and intervention in the telecommunications industry. Briefly, it is the individual ITT subsidiary manager who is responsible for the bulk of strategic and operating decisions. These decisions, however, must be reconciled not only with host governments but also with company headquarters, thus necessitating the establishment of a *dual* negotiations process: between the subsidiary and its host government and between the subsidiary and parent or other subsidiaries. Needless to say, this complicated arrangement has fostered highly institutionalized, formal and informal mechanisms and procedures for both long-term and on-going negotiations.

IBM's emphasis on implicit negotiations and adherence to a centrally developed set of company policies is a direct reflection of the tremendous bargaining strength it enjoys vis-à-vis host governments as a result of its dominant market and technological leadership. In this respect IBM's government-relations strategy can be considered the epitome of the policy-oriented, "pure-type" approach to government-relations management.

The main feature of this policy-oriented strategy is the substantial company trade-offs IBM offers to host governments in key areas of national concern such as investment, trade, and employment. At the same time, however, it explicitly reserves as "nonnegotiable" all questions of ownership and R&D location and control. To encourage government acceptance of these terms IBM publically emphasizes the contributions it can make to the national economy. An example of such a policy is the company's active concern with the ratio of local value-added to local revenues. When this ratio drops following an increase in sales, the host country automatically becomes a priority location for new investments. In other cases IBM offers specific countries ongoing priority with respect to the manufacture of certain kinds of equipment. For example, IBM Deutschland is the company's European base within the EMEA for the manufacture of printers and as such has priority over all investment decisions regarding them.

Another area of IBM's interest in host-government concerns, as outlined in its policy package, is the company's specific attention to the problem of internal trade balance. In general, IBM endeavors to maintain internal trade at a reasonable balance. Whenever the internal-trade balances register a significant deficit, the company seeks to address it in various ways, such as increasing purchases for export from local suppliers or making additional investment in local manufacture. At the same time company policy toward intersubsidiary trade dictates the transfer of products at cost plus a fixed markup in order to avoid complicated transfer pricing issues. Finally, IBM's policy of full employment effectively precludes layoffs of employees in any host country.

The objective of these policies in the negotiating process is twofold: to assure host governments of IBM's commitment to national goals and to demonstrate the substantial contributions the company can make to the country.

It is also important, however, to note the substantial positive benefits that accrue to the company itself in the form of employee loyalty and simplification of investment and sourcing decisions.

In exchange for these "contributions" to the local economy IBM expects to retain its policy of 100% ownership and control over its own operations in its core businesses. Company management justifies this by firmly maintaining that 100% equity is not only good for the customer and in the best interests of the local economy but also equally indispensable for the corporation itself in light of the unique features of the computer industry and the unique characteristics of IBM. In a high-technology, rapidly developing industry the company argues that maximum service at lowest cost can be provided only when manpower and financial resources for development, manufacture, and support are optimized and coordinated on an international basis.

Yet despite these policy proclamations, it is clear that the real issue is one of "power," not "legitimacy." The major benefits of these policies accrue to the company and IBM's unique bargaining strength is their sole guarantor. It is significant to comment in this regard that other high-technology firms have settled for considerably less.

The history of the policy of 100% equity ownership reflects this conscious and deliberate choice of business strategy. Until the late 1950s IBM allowed substantial minority participation in its foreign operations and entered into joint decisions with local partners. In one celebrated case, however, the company was forced to delay the manufacture of a new, highly promising product—the first punch-card machine with magnetic memory—when its conservative U.K. subsidiary partners refused to back it. The realization that local partner's perceptions and interests could diverge so fundamentally from those of headquarters prompted then Chairman Watson to repurchase all noncompany shares in the subsidiary (40% at the time) and initiate a companywide policy of 100% ownership and control.

It should be pointed out that in recent years, because of the pressures of rapid technological development, technological convergence, and enhanced global competition, IBM has entered into a growing number of alliances or joint ventures with U.S. and overseas competitors. These varied alliances are all derived from strategic or tactical considerations like facilitating the company's entry and learning in new product market areas (e.g., IBM's 1983 minority investment in Rolm, a telecommunications company subsequently wholly acquired, and its 1985 minority investment in MCI Communications) or extending its marketing reach (e.g., teaming up with Matsushita to develop a PC for the Japanese market). In no instance has IBM relinquished or shared ownership of its core operations with outsiders under host-government pressure.

The other "nonnegotiable" policy in IBM's government-relations strategy concerns the location and control of its research and development activities. Here, as in other areas, company operations are highly centralized: all product research and development is directly controlled by specialized staff at corporate headquarters, including that which is carried out at its facilities in the United Kingdom, France, and Germany. Decisions regarding the location of new R&D facilities overseas must therefore respond entirely to the economic and scientific attributes of the country involved and not to individual government requests or demands. In the company's view these policies are essential to its pursuit of global integration and a worldwide product strategy.

At the same time, however, IBM has not been able to ignore a host government's concern with national technological development. Interpreting the frequent request for more R&D as part of a natural desire to participate more fully in the technological and scientific revolutions around it, the company has adopted a policy of establishing special "scientific centers" in the countries in which it maintains substantial operations. These centers are specially designed to address the specific needs and concerns of the local environment. For example, IBM is currently engaged in such diverse activities as man-machine communications research in Germany, regional economic modeling in Italy, computer-aided lip reading in France, agricultural modeling in Mexico, and digital radiology in the United Kingdom. In the words of Maisonrouge, former Chairman of IBM Europe/Middle East/Africa:

> While recognizing that our principal role is economic and that our contribution to a given economy is modulated both by the scope of our activities and the host country's particular requirements, we try to look at our total responsibility to the country. That is to say we try to go beyond a minimum level of accountability by contributing more to the community than pure business requirements would dictate. . . .
>
> A substantial part of our contribution is in the form of research conducted in cooperation with universities and national agen-

cies at IBM's scientific centers . . . these centers differ from our
company research laboratories in that their priorities are dictated
by the needs of the communities in which they operate, and not
by the immediate concerns of the firm.[16]

The decision to engage in these Scientific Centers is also centrally made and the cost is seen as a normal cost of doing business.

Like IBM, Ford emphasizes the "long-term" in its dealings
with host governments—primarily to secure a reasonably certain working environment for its large-scale, capital-intensive
investments. But, unlike the implicit "negotiated environment"
of IBM's company policies, the negotiations process for Ford
represents a much more equal match between company and
government bargaining power. Unlike the high-tech computer
business, Ford's automobiles offer no significant technological
or market salience for host governments; and, despite the oligopolistic nature of the industry, competition is such that both
governments and consumers retain a wide range of choice between individual manufacturers. However, what is salient for
national governments is the sheer size and scale of Ford's investments—often representing thousands of jobs and a large
percentage of the country's GNP. Thus company announce-
ments of significant new investment plans often attract considerable international attention and Ford finds itself in the
enviable position of having its business actively solicited by
government officials all over the world. This is especially true
in Europe, where the EEC has fostered a single, integrated automobile market across national boundaries. Here competition for
Ford's business is so keen that it provokes "investment wars"
between the different national governments, each of which offers substantial investment incentives and tax holidays running

[16]Quoted in Y. Doz, *Multinational Strategic Management: Economic and Political Imperatives*, draft, 1980.

into the tens of millions of dollars. (Incentive packages often range in value up to $80 million.) Unlike IBM, whose position in a country is well protected by its technological know-how and market leadership, once Ford decides to invest in a country its bargaining power drops precipitously and its substantial investments become captive guests of the government.

Thus Ford has adopted a negotiations strategy that emphasizes the entry-stage negotiations process when its "quid" commands the highest "quo." The large size and scale of its investments, combined with its highly integrated and rationalized manufacturing network in Europe, makes the company highly vulnerable to renegotiations and incremental adjustments based on new government demands, such as increased exports or increased value-added. Thus Ford's entry-stage negotiations are absolutely crucial for the establishment of a long-term negotiated environment that will permit the company to take full advantage of the "investment wars" while not compromising its long-term security. To achieve this end it must be willing and able to consider substantial trade-offs in the areas of employment, export requirements, and local value-added, particularly in Latin America, where its "quid" isn't very large to begin with.

In the high-growth Third World countries in which Ford operates the biggest prize to be gained in the entry-stage negotiations is simply the right to market access. In exchange for allowing Ford to enter the country, a host government can demand a whole range of company trade-offs on issues such as employment levels, local value-added requirements, and equity participation. In such cases Ford's negotiations strategy is to seek the most secure long-term agreements possible without compromising company freedom and flexibility in key areas. Thus, while agreeing to specific *forms*, it deliberately seeks to retain control over the *substance* of the specific host country requirements. For example, in considering the issue of local value-added requirements, Ford will agree to numerical targets and limits while at the same time insisting on the right to determine independently the specific products and processes to be included. In general, it argues that any restrictions placed on the company should be set at the lowest level in absolute terms and emphasizes the need for graduated time-phased plans for compliance with any new government requirements. Again, its approach is *assertive* and becoming even more so: as a result of the company's experiences in Latin America Ford has been taking an increasingly proactive stance by providing input and expertise in the process of development and formulation of host-country policies in the automotive industry prior to their formal articulation (recent examples: Mexico and Indonesia).

In terms of overall policy objectives, Ford's government-relations strategy is similar to IBM's. Both companies actively promote the "benefits" of 100% equity ownership and control and the "necessity" for retaining company flexibility vis-à-vis national economic and trade regulations.

Unlike IBM, however, the automotive industry, and Ford in particular, is not in a position to impose its policies or preferences on host governments—even in Europe, where it retains substantial bargaining power. As such, Ford must generally settle for less than that for which it aims. What Ford does have, however, is a clear idea of its *relative* bargaining strengths as well as a consistent, well defined strategy for dealing with the inevitable negotiations process. Briefly stated, this strategy has three main objectives: (1) it seeks a long-term agreement that will minimize disruptions to company operations; (2) it has internal guidelines that spell out the company's preferred outcomes; and (3) as part of its long-term agreement it carefully specifies trade-offs that can be incorporated into its overall planning process.

Like IBM and Ford, Eli Lilly also emphasizes a set of specific policy preferences with respect to government issues, but because of the highly regulated nature of the ethical drugs industry it has been forced to adopt a more structured and piecemeal negotiations process for many of the key aspects of its overseas operations. Most countries, particularly in the industrialized world, have established special regulatory agencies and formalized procedures that deal specifically with private companies in this area, with emphasis on the issues of new product registration and introduction, new product pricing, and pricing review of established products. Thus a pharmaceutical company like Eli Lilly has little choice but to enter into negotiations with host governments on decisions that fall within these areas. Because outcomes in these cases are, of necessity, situationally determined by negotiations, Lilly does not have policies in these areas; rather it concentrates on institutionalizing the decision-making authority and the process of company-government interface which determine the shape of the eventual outcomes. Thus, instead of formulating a priori policies, top management concentrates on developing a well defined decision process and then monitoring its operation.

Eli Lilly likes to refer to itself as the "cleanest" company in the world. This is a reference not only to its high medical and hygienic standards but also to its high ethical standards with regard to its business practices. As part of this image, the company has established specific guidelines for company policy on a wide range of issues such as antitrust law, local trade association participation, disclosure of "material" information, and local political contributions, which it publishes in pamphlet form for distribution to all company subsidiary managers.

Given the special sensitivity of most host governments with regard to the issue of pharmaceutical transfer pricing (and given the difficulty of "arm's-length" pricing due to the lack of comparable products in the international market), Eli Lilly has instituted a policy of uniform transfer pricing worldwide; that is, a single-transfer price is used for a drug in intersubsidiary trade, irrespective of the country destination and its tax and import duties structure. By offering the consistency and comparability of its prices in all 130 countries in which it operates as a guarantee of its own good faith, the company seeks to defend its own pricing policies in government negotiations. At the same time the company has proved to be cognizant and respectful of other government concerns, such as employment and local value-added. Like IBM, it pursues a policy of full employment and, like Ford, it stresses the contributions of its local manufacturing and finishing plants as an important element in local value-added.

Though also classified as an assertive company, ITT pursues a very different approach to government-relations management than the other three. To begin with, ITT's pursuit of a country-oriented strategy itself reflects a fundamental adaptation to the realities of government power and dominance over the national industry markets. ITT's country-oriented strategy reflects an extreme manifestation of national responsiveness. Having adopted this strategic posture, how can one describe its ongoing management of government relations?

Briefly, ITT's government-relations strategy can be defined as one of "proactive national accommodation." Given the primacy of government purchasing power in the telecommunications field, not to mention the existence of highly segmented national markets, this in effect means that each country manager must reach an understanding with his host government over the whole range of issues that is normally negotiated by the company as a whole, including the nature and extent of local R&D, new product specifications, manufacturing technology, investment, exports, and local value-added. As an integral part of this strategy, ITT encourages each subsidiary to seek government grants and subsidies actively (in recent years this support has represented an important portion of ITT investments, as in the case of ITT's U.K. subsidiary, Standard Telephone and Cables, in its development of System X—the all-electronic exchange system).

ITT specifically pursues policies that are designed to facilitate the country orientation of its subsidiaries. For example, in the ITT network country management has become the center of initiative on all resource allocation and R&D issues through such companywide policies as self-sufficiency in the local manufacture of products and R&D expenditures, arms-length pricing, and the avoidance of centralized foreign exchange management. In a similar vein ITT's foreign operations rarely bear the ITT name, and in some cases its subsidiaries are even listed on the local stock exchange.

Despite this emphasis on subsidiary autonomy, however, ITT country managers remain accountable to corporate headquarters, and the commitments they enter into are carefully monitored by a system of monthly meetings and peer review to ensure their incorporation into the overall company plan.

In sum, ITT's government-relations strategy involves an offer of a nationally responsive subsidiary geared toward serving the needs of their national markets in return for continued preferential treatment by the government side. Yet mere responsiveness does not provide a guarantee for the performance of this exchange. The real levers that ITT country managers use to ensure their survival and growth are access to technology (via ITT's large and varied, though somewhat fragmented, R&D network) and export markets (provided by the wide geographic spread of the company). Use of these strengths in a proactive, anticipatory way in periodic negotiations is what differentiates ITT subsidiaries as partners in their local industries from hapless supplicants.

As illustrated by the preceding examples, all four companies in the Assertive Mode base their government-relations strategies on a keen sensitivity to the interests and concerns of host governments as well as on an awareness of the potential regulatory and purchasing power they wield over their industries. This has translated at the negotiating table into a necessity for compromise and a willingness to accommodate. At the same time, however, these companies are equally cognizant of their own need to retain a certain strategic independence and integrity for survival.

Companies pursuing an assertive approach to foreign governments generally seek to establish a long-term concord, whether formal or informal, in which government concerns can be met without compromising the strategic independence and integrity of the firm. By reducing the uncertainty this "negotiated environment" greatly facilitates the planning process. This is especially important for companies that pursue a strategy of worldwide integration, such as IBM, Ford, and Eli Lilly; however, it has also proved to be very important for companies like ITT that pursue a country-specific approach to operations. Here, the establishment of a negotiated environment at the individual country level achieves essentially the same objectives of reducing uncertainty and obtaining the most favorable trade-offs for the company.

GOVERNMENT-RELATIONS PROCESS

In this section we examine two distinct sets of processes involving the interaction between subunits within a firm: (1) the process of internal corporate response to government issues and (2) the process of interaction between the company and the host government. In both cases we emphasize the systematic differences between the roles of managers at different levels and across different issues.

The nature of the issues involved in the management of government relations can be classified according to (1) their overall importance to the firm and (2) the extent of their impact on the various subunits within it. By "important" issues we are generally referring to major strategic concerns of the company, such as investment decisions, which have wide resource allocation implications, and the ownership policies, which have direct bearing on its control stakes. These important issues are typically discrete and infrequent in occurrence and their impact on the firm is usually direct, immediate, and highly visible. By "extent of impact," or reach, of an issue we are referring to the nature and number of subunits affected. For example, when an issue involving interdependent subunits or functional staff arises *within* a specific area or division, its scope is defined as *narrow* and it is generally resolved within the regular structure of a firm. However, when an issue requires special coordination *between* regions or differentiated subunits within a firm, its impact can be described as *broad*, and various temporary structures, such as extrastructural mechanisms (e.g., temporary task forces or project teams), are established to forge the necessary links and build the necessary consensus.

Internal Response Process

The most frequent government issues that confront a large multinational company are narrow in reach in that they affect primarily interdependent subunits grouped under an area management. Affecting, as they do, the normal strategic and operating decisions of the particular area or region in which they developed, these issues are dealt with typically in a routine manner within the regular structure of the firm, rising to the specific functional or area-level management that has authority over all the subunits involved, as would other nongovernmental issues.

For example, in Ford's initial negotiations for new investments in Spain, Portugal, and the United Kingdom the responsibility for developing specific company positions on issues such as exports, production levels, and value-added lay with the functional staffs at Ford of Europe headquarters in England. The primary consideration here, of course, was the area-wide impact of these policies on the company's highly integrated European market. At the same time, however, Ford of Europe headquarters was often called on to assume responsibility for more local issues, particularly when the latter threatened to have cross-border repercussions. For example, the Ford of Europe staff closely followed the periodic negotiations of its British subsidiary with the labor unions, though subsidiary management was responsible for policy and the handling of labor negotiations. But when, in the fall of 1978, an eight-week strike at Ford-U.K. plants threatened to compromise manufacturing operations all over Europe, it was the functional staffs at Ford of Europe headquarters—not the local plant management—that intervened and authorized the final settlement. What is significant to note in this instance is that the ensuing labor contract with British workers was far in excess of both local management recommendations and British government industrial relations policy. Through this internal process of "leveling up" important issues Ford has been able to ensure a companywide perspective on the outcome. In this case it was decided that the cost of a strike would be greater than the risk of government sanctions—or even poor profit margins in the U.K. subsidiary.

Decisions on pricing a new drug product in overseas markets are among the most delicate and difficult in the pharmaceutical business. Pricing of new drugs in the country of the first introduction tends to set a benchmark for permissible prices in other countries at the time of subsequent introduction as well as a base for future price increases. Within the formal organization structure of Eli Lilly general responsibility for pricing issues falls to the Central Marketing Staff of the Domestic Pharmaceutical Division which has a worldwide product-planning mandate. However, the need to take into account the policies of national pricing boards and the differences in government sensitivities toward new drug pricing led to the formation of a special committee, outside the regular corporate structure, which brings together area executives from the international division and the central marketing staffs. This special committee is charged with reviewing proposed new drug pricing. Area executives are thus able to bring to bear their intimate knowledge of a country's regulatory environment to the global functional perspective of the staff on such cases. The result is the development of an acceptable price range for each country, thus permitting country managers flexibility in adjusting to the stringency of the particular national policy environment.

The handling of other key government issues that have been incorporated into Lilly's regular corporate structure include (1) the provision of scientific and technical evidence to meet national product registration standards and (2) the positioning of new products. Again, it is primarily the Corporate Research and Development Staff and the Central Marketing Staff that oversee these functions. For example, when a new product is ready for market, the corporate R&D staff compiles a general "product registration package" that consists of all relevant scientific, technical, and pricing information which is then sent out to the individual product registration specialists in the country subsidiaries for presentation to host-country regulatory agencies.

Given the large amounts of information required by government health authorities and specialized intergovernmental organizations such as WHO, which facilitates information and experience exchange among national authorities, it is becoming increasingly important for drug companies to promote a consistent global image. This consistency not only ensures company credibility but also greatly simplifies clearance procedures. For example, when a new product passes government approval in one country, other countries are likely to follow suit. As such, it is not surprising that global product-positioning decisions are handled by the Corporate Marketing Staffs.

When a government issue extends beyond the subunits within a particular area or affects the activities of differentiated functional groups between regions, the most frequent response of a large MNC is to create an intersubsidiary or interregional task force or standing committee that is external to the regular structure of the firm. These extrastructural mechanisms are specifically designed to forge the necessary lateral links between the affected units; and it is only in the event of the nonresolution of an issue that problems climb up the organization ladder to the division or corporate level.

For example, in Ford's International Automotive Operations coordination between regions is frequently referred to a special Business Planning Staff attached to the office of the Executive Vice President of the International Automotive Operations. This staff deals primarily with those issues that occur in response to new government demands in one country or region that affects the operations of subsidiaries in another—for instance, the request by Brazilian authorities for an increase in company export quotas in the late 1970s which necessitated a reallocation of export markets beyond Latin America. The Business Planning Staff brought the executives of different areas together to deal with the situation.

Another dramatic example of Ford's use of extrastructural task forces occurred during a recent controversy that pitted one major division against another. In response to a direct Mexican government requirement for the local manufacture of engines for all automotive producers in the country Ford's Latin American division and its Mexican subsidiary teamed up to promote the construction of a $365-million, 400,000-unit engine plant in Mexico to serve the North American market. Because at that time the North American Automotive Operations (which is a separate operation, distinct from the other regional operations that come under the formal umbrella of Ford's International Automotive Operations) had been gearing up for a similar investment proposal for its operations in Cleveland (where an idle V-8 engine facility was scheduled for conversion to a 400,000-unit, 2.2-liter, I-4 engine plant for the U.S. market), in essence the Latin American regional management proposal meant a transfer of this major investment project to Mexico.

This situation led to a confrontation between the Latin American and North American divisions: the former argued for the lower factor costs and higher market growth potential of Mexico and emphasized the fact that the credits generated by exports of locally produced engines would be crucial toward meeting the other major government requirement of company balance of trade; the latter countered by highlighting the political fallout for "exporting jobs," the inadequacy of Mexican infrastructure, and lower productivity of Mexican labor. Faced with this seemingly irreconcilable difference between two of its major divisions, Ford senior management formed a special task force under the leadership of the powerful Corporate Strategy Staff to which they invited senior managers from both sides of the controversy as well as various corporate and regional functional staff members. With all relevant actors participating, responsibility for guiding the group toward a final decision was vested in the hands of the CSS leadership to ensure that companywide interests would prevail. The decision was to invest in Mexico.

Eli Lilly made constant use of a special intercorporate standing committee to resolve the delicate and highly political issue of drug transfer pricing. This committee met monthly and was composed of the President of the International Division, the heads of the three area subdivisions within International, the Corporate Vice-Presidents of Pharmaceutical and Agricultural Divisions, Legal Counsel, the Director of Corporate Tax Staff, and the International Finance Staff. Transfers within the Lilly network amounted to nearly $350 million, or 35% of international sales. This Standing Committee met monthly and was responsible for making adjustments in the company policy of uniform worldwide transfer prices.

At ITT the use of special committees, joint task forces, and working groups outside the regular corporate structure is much more extensive and widespread than in any of the other companies studied. This is primarily because of its country-oriented approach to international operations and the consequent necessity for coordinating decisions of interest with other subsidiaries to ensure companywide interests. Regular monthly meetings between country managers consider such strategic questions as the allocation of R&D activities and export contract responsibility. At the same time these monthly meetings provide a forum for shifts in strategy to take advantage of changing international

and financial relations. For example, at one meeting it was decided to shift the negotiating responsibility for a major contract
with Algeria from France to Spain, when Franco-Algerian relations soured on immigration issues and the future of the Spanish Sahara. Spain, aligned with the Algerian position, was a
much more suitable base for negotiations. Once the contract
had been secured, however, ITT managers decided to source a
substantial part of the contract from the French subsidiary via
Spain, thus soothing the French government's ruffled feelings.

Another example of this type of informal collective decision
making among ITT subsidiary managers occurs during the initial stages of an export contract negotiation. Rather than bidding
individually for a client's business, potential customers are directed from one subsidiary to the next and thus are allowed to
see and evaluate various equipment lines before making their
decisions. Once the customer's choice has been made, however,
the responsibility falls entirely on the chosen manufacturer.

ITT has also instituted some formal mechanisms to facilitate
this information-coordination process. For example, it has established a Special Technical Staff Department attached to ITT-
Europe headquarters in Brussels to aid in intersubsidiary coordination on technical and R&D issues. It is significant to note
that this department has been given no direct authority over local decision making.

Major investment decisions are the most obvious class of issues to be considered by top management. At Ford the importance of these decisions is further enhanced by the situation of
project "bids" from more than one government—particularly in
Europe, where the EEC has fostered a single integrated market.
Here, each regional and country subunit is responsible for its
own proposal and must lay the groundwork and do all feasibility studies required for the promotion of its own country as an
investment site. The overall importance of these "lumpy" investments to company operations, however, necessitates close
involvement of senior management in the final decision stages.

Another class of issues that is of particular concern to senior management contains those that are exceptions to company policy and guidelines. Top-level consideration of policy deviations is especially important at IBM, where the company policy framework for dealing with foreign governments is all-important. As with most issues that rise to the top within IBM, issues involving possible exception to government-relations policy are reviewed by the Corporate Management Board (CMB) which is comprised of the top five corporate executives. A poignant example of the role and response of this committee occurred during the mid-1970s when the Indian government informed the company that it would have to reduce its 100% equity ownership to 40% in accordance with the Foreign Investment Review Act. IBM's Indian operations were relatively small, with only 800 employees, and of only marginal significance to overall company operations. Moreover, far from the high-tech "leading company" image it liked to portray, IBM-India was primarily engaged in the rather mundane reconditioning of used computers for the Indian market and at one point the manufacture of simple keypunch machines for export. Nevertheless, despite the arguments on the Indian side, IBM top management feared the precedent-setting impact of acquiescence and spent considerable time formulating a response that would obviate the necessity for compromise. After three years of deliberation a proposal that consisted of the following revisions to company policy was finally presented to the government: Indian operations were to be divided into two companies—one to be 40% IBM-owned to serve essentially as a service bureau and the other, in which IBM would retain full ownership, to handle all marketing, maintenance, and manufacturing operations. In keeping with Indian law the latter would produce primarily for export, and, as a concession to government concern with local R&D, IBM offered to establish government-owned, company-operated testing labs and research centers; finally, the company would make certain IBM patents available to Indian enterprises. This proposal was subsequently rejected by the Indian government, thus forcing IBM to withdraw. This was followed shortly by IBM's withdrawal from Nigeria over the same ownership question.

What is significant to note here is not the proposal itself but rather the significant amount of top management time devoted to it. The fear of a precedent-setting compromise on a fundamental issue of company policy kept senior management attention focused on its insignificant Indian operations for more than four years.

Explanations of the failure of the Indian negotiations reveal the specific weaknesses and strengths of this type of centrally developed policy approach to government-relations management: to begin with, the time involved in formulating an appropriate response to government pressures points to a dangerous inflexibility. A rapidly changing world requires continual policy review and revision; yet, where policy is all-important, any change has immediate system-wide repercussions. This has the effect of frustrating even the most incremental adjustments to company policy.

Thus IBM's initial emphasis on exemption from Indian law—combined with the particularly long lead time in formulating its response—had the effect of damaging the company's credibility in the government's eyes. It also gave the government the time and the incentive to cultivate other options (by 1977 at least two companies, Burroughs and International Computer Ltd., had agreed to joint ventures with majority local ownership).

At the same time, however, it is significant to note the importance of the learning process involved in this careful and detailed weighing of corporate priorities, especially on a "global" issue such as ownership, to IBM as a whole. In the process of developing a viable alternative proposal that would revise rather than rewrite company policy IBM was able to anticipate similar demands from other governments. In many respects, however, the considerable time and effort devoted to fashioning

a response to the Indian case and the question of equity ownership in highly regulated economies may merely postpone the
inevitable victory of host-government policy in this area; yet,
company management at IBM evidently believed that even a
few extra years of company control would have made the effort
worthwhile. In this respect it is important to note that the re-
vised policy was subsequently used in IBM negotiations with
both Indonesia and Malaysia—with considerably more success.
IBM has permitted local ownership of IBM agencies for marketing and service in these countries.

Within the multinational companies in our sample issues regarding important intergovernmental negotiations bearing on
company interests were generally referred to a permanent Government Affairs Staff or a semipermanent full-time specialized
task force under a senior corporate executive.

Operating within the context of a global system of nation
states, MNCs must continually be aware of international negotiations and agreements between governments that bear on their
interests. Most significant, of course, are the multilateral treaties between governments that incorporate international law
into municipal law with direct and enforceable results. These
treaties are generally concerned with questions of industrial
regulation, trade policies, and so on, but even in the more ambiguous realm of international law and multilateral organizations companies are careful to follow the currents of international public opinion.

IBM, for example, is very concerned with the different national regulatory regimes that are currently seeking to regulate
transborder data flows. In an effort to influence national policy
makers and present company positions to the international conferences, IBM has established a full-time, single-issue task force
on transborder data flows under the direction of a corporate
vice president at company headquarters in Armonk, New York.

Ford's International Government Affairs staff also operates
out of company headquarters in Dearborn, Michigan, and has

specific responsibility for developing company positions on issues such as talks on revisions to the U.S.-Canada Automotive
Products Trade Agreement between the two governments.

Finally, the Government Affairs Staff of Eli Lilly was particularly active in the early 1980s in the reversal of a WHO Advisory Group recommendation to place the drug Darvon on the restricted narcotics list. In this instance the company formed a
special task force under the direction of the Government Affairs
Staff, which included geographic and functional managers from
all regional divisions. This task force worked for six months to
mobilize international support for the drug, coordinating its efforts between the international organizations and the national
health authorities who participated in the WHO decision. The
successful reconsideration of the ban represented a significant
achievement of this group and lent substantial support to the
arguments for a more anticipatory, coordinated approach to international issues. This particular event resulted in the creation
of an ongoing monitoring role for Lilly's Government Affairs
Staff in this area.

Company-Government Interface

In all four companies studied the decision as to who actually
negotiates with government officials also seems to reflect the
broad nature and the importance of the issues. For example,
when an issue requires a major investment decision, it is generally top management that steps in, whereas when the concern is
only a local requirement for more value-added it is generally
the local managers who conduct the discussion.

Other systematic variations in the roles played by different
levels of management vis-à-vis company-government interface
can be seen at different stages of the negotiations life cycle or
according to the perceptions of the importance of the particular
country involved.

One of the major reasons for the involvement of senior management in company-government negotiations is the government concern with prestige. Government officials often view country managers of integrated multinationals as poor substitutes for the "real" company decision makers and frequently insist that corporate line executives lead the negotiations. On several occasions in the last decade Henry Ford II himself led the company negotiations team for new investments in Europe. In 1979, for example, Ford chaired a high-level team that was engaged in highly publicized negotiations with Austria, France, Portugal, and Spain. To some extent this was a function of the attention given to such investments by the very highest levels of the governments involved in addition to the intrinsic importance of a major investment project to the company. Unemployment in France and Portugal, forthcoming elections in Austria, and regional development concerns in Spain made all four candidates eager to win Ford's favor and quick to publicize the negotiations process, playing up their own possibilities for selection. Prior to the "high-level" negotiations most of the technical and economic groundwork had been laid by government and bureaucrats and area staff groups; however, it was Ford who negotiated with the heads of governments. When Portugal was tentatively selected as the investment site, the company sent Phillip Caldwell, its then President, to mend ill feelings and avoid potential misunderstandings with the other governments. This proved to be particularly important, for subsequent economic hardships caused the company to postpone all new European investments.

In some situations the involvement of senior management is designed especially to indicate the seriousness of company intent and commitment toward the country and project. For example, in conjunction with IBM's proposals for a significant expansion of its operations in Mexico, Ralph Pfeiffer, Chairman of the IBM Americas/Far East Corporation, met personally with the President of Mexico to resolve some outstanding issues and officially seal the understanding at the highest level. This was especially important because IBM was seeking specific exemption from local ownership laws.

Senior management may also become involved in the negotiations process in order to resolve problems that appear farther down the line. For instance, after failing to secure what he considered to be fair pricing increases in France a senior executive of Eli Lilly spent an entire week in Paris arguing the company's point of view—without immediate success. At another time a member of Lilly's top management was sent to Brazil to negotiate import license assurances for its new $15-million joint-venture agricultural chemicals project. In this case also, despite convincing arguments on the company's behalf, the effort was unsuccessful.

In some cases corporate top management also responds to its own perceptions of prestige—often unrelated to the underlying economic or strategic importance of an issue. For example, the rush of American multinationals to establish footholds in the Chinese market (PRC) was, in many cases, masterminded by company chairmen as their pet projects. In any other case an issue like that would normally be referred to an area line executive.

Finally, senior management has often become directly engaged in major divestment negotiations, as in 1976 when ITT was pressured by the French government into selling part of its operations to Thompson CSF, a domestic firm. In this case senior corporate managers not only developed guidelines for their subsidiary management but were also themselves involved in the negotiations.

In the ongoing effort to conserve top management time and talent several companies in our sample have sought specifically to emphasize the credibility of area executives. For example, both IBM's EMEA and Ford's European Area management are currently viewed by host governments as full-fledged negotiating partners and as such are able to shoulder the major responsibility for government issues affecting their operations.

Moreover, wherever company strategy is necessarily focused on individual country markets, as it is in Latin America whose government policies discourage market integration, these companies emphasize local subsidiary management credibility and responsibility in government relations. Whereas in Europe country managers tend to be essentially marketing managers, in Latin America they are more often considered as general managers with responsibilities for manufacturing operations as well. Thus each Latin American country subsidiary has its own functional staffs, with the staff attached to the Latin American regional headquarters performing oversight and administrative roles.

In all four companies observed it was primarily the country-level subsidiary managers who served as the first line of communication with host governments. In this ongoing role they are primarily responsible for maintaining contact with the appropriate authorities, for clarifying government demands or requests, and for presenting the company position on specific issues. These responsibilities, of course, are in addition to the normal duties of good corporate citizenship within a country, such as compliance with all local laws and regulations on issues of worker safety and environmental protection. Often a small staff is specifically set aside to deal with them.

In those countries in which governments are specially organized to deal with MNCs the company subsidiary generally displays a corresponding specialized staff structure for handling them. This is particularly true in the pharmaceutical industry, as illustrated by the maintenance of full-time product registration specialists in many of Lilly's country subsidiaries. Though these staffs generally rely on specific R&D directives and advice from corporate headquarters, they also have the responsibility for maintaining close contact with national regulations, for laying the groundwork for company submission on its products and prices, and for answering any bureaucratic follow-ups that might be necessary.

So far we have dealt with instances of direct contact and negotiations between the company and government. In some cases, however, the parties may communicate with each other indirectly by using public pronouncements of their positions or concerns to signal the other party. In one case the subsidiary manager of IBM-France warned publicly that should the French government extend the time for assistance to CII-HB beyond the original period to which it had agreed IBM would reconsider its planned new investments in the country. Government officials publicly responded by denying that government purchasing policy guidelines discriminated against IBM and that companies (including state-owned firms) were free to select their own suppliers. By late 1979, however, despite the lack of serious direct contact between the parties, it was clear that the government was no longer helping CII-HB to the same extent. Clearly such situations are the exception rather than the rule. IBM had the privilege of parlaying its strengths and unique position within the industry into novel forms of interaction with the government. Few, if any, other companies could afford to adopt a similar stance.

As we have seen before, ITT places almost exclusive emphasis on its country managers for government issues and negotiations. Generally, it is the subsidiary manager of ITT Telecommunications Equipment Operations who coordinates and controls company-government relations for all other ITT product divisions within a country.

An extreme form of handling the company-government interface is the centralization of all dealings with certain governments in one office. This is especially true of company relations with the communist governments of Eastern Europe. For example, both IBM and Lilly centralized their dealings with the communist bloc in special offices based in Vienna. This was deemed necessary in order to respond effectively to the dominance of state-owned companies and centralized bureaucracies in Eastern Europe and to ensure strict compliance with U.S. trade and investment laws in that area.

Finally, in a few cases companies actually worked together in their dealings with foreign host governments. Again, this was especially true for the pharmaceutical companies, in which the heavy involvement of government lends a certain uniformity of form and substance to the problems that confront all companies in the industry. For example, in Latin America, where the entire pharmaceutical industry is foreign-owned, MNCs frequently hire internationally recognized accounting and auditing firms, such as Price Waterhouse, through the local pharmaceutical industry associations to conduct industry-wide profitability and pricing studies. The companies then present these reports collectively to host governments as a means of justifying their individual pricing policies. In some cases the U.S. Pharmaceutical Manufacturers Association is used as a forum by U.S.-based drug companies to intercede with foreign governments on behalf of industry-wide issues and to assist in the development of local trade associations.

GOVERNMENT-RELATIONS STRUCTURE

In light of the tremendous range and variety of issues that affect the relations between MNCs and foreign governments, it is almost impossible to single out a specific government-relations function from the myriad of functional concerns that bear on the management of an international network. The management of government relations must therefore be viewed as an ongoing process that cuts across all functional and organizational hierarchies and affects all of a firm's strategic, operational, and structural choices.

The structure for management of government relations extends beyond the regular or formal organizational structure of a firm to involve functional, geographic, or product divisions and hierarchical levels of management. It includes extrastructural mechanisms that are used to form temporary or permanent links between otherwise unrelated subunits and levels of management, specialized government-affairs staff, and the "structural context" of the individual firm.

As in the specific organizational processes for the management of government relations, the structure for management of government issues also tends to reflect the importance and/or reach of the specific issue. The impact of the same issue may be narrow or broad, depending on the location of the affected units within the firm's formal structure. The reach of issues may be said to be narrow when it affects closely interdependent units or functions; the reach is defined as broad when it affects highly differentiated units.

In general, whenever issues relate to interdependent subsidiaries or functions that correspond to the primary dimension along which the firm is formally organized, responsibility for managing these issues is usually designated by the formal structure of the firm. For example, in an integrated MNC network, which is organized by area divisions such as IBM or Ford, government issues (e.g., exports) arising in, say, Spain, which affect other subsidiaries in Europe (but not those outside), are generally dealt with by the European Area Functional Staffs, whose writ for coordination of such issues extends areawide. When, as in IBM and Ford, the research and development function is centralized at the corporate level, all government issues pertaining to R&D, irrespective of the country or area in which they originate, are handled by the corporate R&D staff whose mandate is worldwide.

In such instances the formal organization structure by itself suffices to provide the structure for the firm's management of government relations. As such, the specific routine responsibility for different issues will lie with different functional staffs or line executives within whose expertise or field of authority they lie.

When, however, the reach of an issue is broad, that is, it affects differentiated units or functions located in different divisions defined by the formal structure or at different levels within the corporate hierarchy, then the formal organization no longer defines the structure for management of government relations. For management of issues with broad impact *extrastructural mechanisms*, such as ad hoc or formal task forces, working parties, project teams, and committees are created to forge the necessary lateral links between the differentiated units.

For example, if, as at Ford-Brazil, the commitments for export demanded by the government cannot be contained within the Latin American region but affect markets in Africa currently sourced from Europe, then extrastructural mechanisms are called for to establish links between the two separate divisions and to resolve their conflicting interests. The Business Planning staff attached to Ford's International Automotive Operations helped to create a joint task force, comprised of executives and staff from the two regional divisions, that resulted in the reallocation of export markets to each division. Thus the principal reason for the use of extrastructural mechanisms is to overcome the high communications barriers between divisions and to facilitate the difficult task of coordination of the activities of foreign subsidiaries in different divisions.

Whereas companies in the assertive mode have a generally anticipatory posture toward government issues, the reach of the specific issue cannot be adequately foreseen. The variety of circumstances surrounding an issue that might determine its reach makes this anticipation difficult. As such, top management cannot legislate the assignment of decision-making responsibilities or define procedure to cover various contingencies. Consequently the use of extrastructural mechanisms is a real-time decision made once the reach of an issue has been determined.

Whether extrastructural mechanisms created are ad hoc and situation-specific in nature or have a longer tenure depends on how frequently a specific issue is encountered and how enduring its effects. For example, the task force created to resolve the location of a major engine-plant investment sought by both the

North American and Latin American divisions is an example of an ad hoc temporary mechanism for dealing with a specific issue that is unlikely to be repeated. However, Lilly's establishment of a standing committee of geographic, functional, and product managers to deal with transfer pricing issues is a testimony to the frequency with which such questions are posed and the potentially serious consequences that an individual case in this issue-area can have.

The use of extrastructural mechanisms alleviates the need for top management to engage directly in substantive decision making or decision arbitration except on important issues. For multinationals in salient industries operating in a large number of countries the sheer volume and complexity of decisions being forced on them for resolution (in the absence of extrastructural mechanisms) would soon result in top-management overload, tax the firm's information system, and vitiate the generation of commitment from the affected parties in implementing decisions in the making of which they had played no role. The development of overlaid temporary structures and processes permits the interpretation of the interests of differentiated units to take place by the participation of the affected units themselves rather than by senior managers located in the corporate hierarchy. In creating these temporary mechanisms, top management focuses on influencing the decision process by designing the necessary link between groups that must deal with the particular case or class of decisions.

For some decisions geographic, product, and functional managers must all be involved. For others some managers may be assigned added responsibility and power.

In making use of temporary structures and mechanisms to complement the formal structure in the management of government relations, top management concentrates on the input side of the decision process instead of being concerned with decision outputs. However, by influencing the composition and leadership of task forces they can reflect corporate goals and priorities while at the same time providing managers who represent divergent points of view an opportunity to resolve their differences and reach joint decisions to which they can feel committed. The existence of internal policy guidelines on government issues in these companies helps to ensure that the joint decisions reached are consistent with company policies.

Assertive companies in this study tend to have a formal government-affairs staff function, though differences in size, locus in the organizational hierarchy, and roles of special staffs across companies are considerable. Their involvement in, and contribution to, the company's management of government relations, however, can be characterized as marginal at best.

At Ford specialized government-affairs staff are located at corporate and regional headquarters and in major country subsidiaries, such as Mexico and Brazil. At IBM an "external-affairs staff" is attached to the Area Divisions and major subsidiaries. These staff groups are small in size, usually numbering between 10 and 15 persons at area or corporate headquarters; in country subsidiaries where the function exists it typically involves only one or two persons. At Lilly the government-affairs staff is primarily U.S.-oriented.

The roles played by these specialized affairs staffs are varied. Their primary role is an advisory one to senior management at the corporate or regional level. Frequently they are responsible for conducting broad country political environment studies, and they assist management in dealing with international organizations, like the UN and ILO, on issues such as the evolving codes of conduct for MNCs or in following developments in the Arab Boycott. Only rarely are these staffs involved in policy making or oversight responsibility for a particular issue. At Ford the international government-affairs staff was designated as the lead staff in coordinating Ford's policy posture toward revisions of the U.S.-Canada Auto Pact and in monitoring Ford's compliance with the Sullivan Principles concerning labor relations in South Africa. Only at IBM, and then as part of

IBM's formal conflict resolution process, does the specialized staff have the right to "nonconcurrence" with decisions made by line units with respect to government issues.

The limited role of these staffs in the firm's government-relations management structure is a reflection of their lack of expertise or their authority over the kind of strategic and operating decisions that are affected by government demands. Moreover, because such staffs were born only in the late 1970s, the function is embryonic and still trying to establish credibility and gain acceptance with other functions in the company.

Finally, the management of government relations is often facilitated by the specific "structural-context" factors of the firm. Bower developed the concept to explain how various decisions distributed within the organization could be made into a consistent whole. He described context as follows:

> Context shapes the purposive manager's definition of business problems by directing, delimiting, and coloring the focus and perception; it determines the priorities which the various demands on him are given.

Context thus goes beyond the lines of the hierarchical organization to include planning and budgeting systems, information flow and systems, career paths, and control and measurement systems for managers. By shaping the perceptions of external events and structuring the priorities of managers, context strongly influences future choices. Bower argues the need to intergrate phases in the strategic process to ensure "consistency along the multiple dimensions of strategy and structure of the initiating parts and the corporate whole."[17]

A distinctive feature of companies in the assertive mode is the extent to which corporate management has shaped the structural context of their firms to reflect their conscious and

[17]Joseph L. Bower, *Managing the Resource Allocation Process*, Harvard Business School Division of Research, Boston, 1970.

deliberate emphasis on the facilitation of government-issues management: throughout the system issues are permitted to surface early and specific mechanisms and processes are instituted to effect their resolution within and between different levels of management.

An entire study could be undertaken on the subject of how and to what extent a firm's administrative systems facilitate the implementation of a selected government-relations strategy or mode. Given the broader objective of this research in developing an understanding of a company's overall approach toward management of government relations, administrative systems were but one of the many aspects covered. Here I briefly examine the elements of the structural context as they affect government-relations management: specifically, (1) planning and budgeting systems, (2) conflict resolution systems, (3) channels for transfer of experience, and (4) corporate culture of the four firms in our sample.

Planning and Budgeting

The formal planning and budgeting systems of a multinational corporation provide important channels for the incorporation of lower management goals and objectives into the overall strategic plans of the firm. The process of reconciling the divergent views into a single blueprint for company action is especially important in integrated companies, where the bulk of planning and budgeting decisions must necessarily be made at the corporate level.

Input on government-relations issues from area and country management takes two basic forms: (1) "environmental strategies" to accommodate individual national laws and other changes in the local environment and (2) "functional strategies" aimed at improving individual subsidiary-government relations and the expansion of local operations. An environmental strategy, for example, includes such company-government issues as worker codetermination laws or South African employment practices, whereas a functional strategy revolves around parent-subsidiary issues and generally incorporates the individual manager's desire for more attention from headquarters (e.g., a new investment project). When capacity planning decisions are centrally controlled, the effect of functional strategy recommendations frequently pit one country subsidiary against another as they vie for limited funds.

To ensure that country initiatives are not ignored by corporate staffs, who may oppose them on economic grounds, subsidiary managers are encouraged to raise such issues directly with top management. At IBM decisions to risk losing some government business or to risk having excess capacity locked in the country are made by the Corporate Management Board.

At ITT individual country managers are essentially free to set their own plans and budgets. Here the reconciliation process must be "bottom up" rather than "top down," with senior management acting as participants and advisors rather than as designers and decision makers. The institutional mechanisms in this process consist of an elaborate and highly formalized information and control system combined with the regular monthly meetings between subsidiary managers at which each country manager must be prepared to defend his own plans to the smallest detail.

Conflict Resolution

As discussed in the preceding section, a distinguishing feature of the Assertive companies studied is the extent to which they use extrastructural mechanisms in the resolution of internal conflicts as a result of government issues. It is also interesting to examine the extent to which existing firm conflict-resolution systems and processes are geared toward management of government issues.

IBM has established a formal and structured system known

as "confrontation process" to encourage resolution of intersubsidiary or interunit conflicts by middle managers. This system basically allows individual managers from any operating or staff subunit to voice objections to the plans and budgets of any other subunit whose activities specifically affect them. As part of this process the dissenting subunit is entitled to demand the formation of a joint working party to resolve the issue. Should this working party fail to reach a reasonable agreement, contending parties can then duly register their differences in a formal "nonconcurrency" vote on the company budgeting decisions. This automatically opens the issue for consideration by a higher level of management. Needless to say, this nonconcurrence mechanism is not often used for fear of losing credibility; it is true, however, that each year more than 200 of these votes of dissension eventually reach the corporate level for final arbitration. As a final stage in the process the CMB usually sets up a new high-level working party under the chairmanship of a senior executive of a major operating unit. By allowing all levels of management to air their grievances formally in this manner this "contention process" of issue resolution at IBM has the effect of encouraging subsidiary managers to take an active interest in company-wide concerns and to work toward a balance between local and global interests within the company. In one instance the area external-affairs staff successfully challenged a line management recommendation to cease operations in a country because of the onerous trading and operating regulations—and prevailed.

To counterbalance the company-wide bias toward subsidiary autonomy top management at ITT has encouraged the development of a strong esprit de corps among subsidiary managers. An important component of this process subjects the plans and resource allocation budgets of each subsidiary to peer approval. Peer control takes place at two levels: at informal regular meetings of the powerful heads of major telecommunications equipment subsidiaries and at large, formal, monthly meetings attended by top management and corporate staffs. Harold Geneen, the redoubtable Chairman of ITT for nearly two decades, characterized the process in the following words:

> We learned to communicate. That's not talking on a telephone. We must spend close to 60 days, long days, each year in these European meetings; and we talk in detail about our problems. We cover the entire range of our activities: production design, delivery, markets, new products, and so forth. And we include the environment; that is, the surrounding social, political, and economic situations.
>
> Do this for 10-11 years, and you have a mass volume of communications. You can't even begin to understand what we mean by communications, unless you consider the sum total of all that information, and all that exchange of detail. We really begin to understand how each of us thinks. We became a group, dealing together with problems. And this problem orientation means that our meetings are pointed; we don't waste time.
>
> We insist that problems be put out in the open. Our working rules are designed to achieve this. For example, anybody on our staff can go anywhere in the company and ask questions. If he has criticisms, he must bring them up with the plant manager. There's none of this hidden-ball stuff. If they can't agree, they go up the ladder.
>
> By operating this way, we cut through three layers of management. At other firms, everyone is careful about their recommendations, and then committees consider them, and reports are filed and discussed. By the time a proposal reaches the top guy, he doesn't know what it means.[18]

Thus, although much more informal and ad hoc than IBM's, ITT's system is no less extensive.

Unlike IBM and ITT, Ford did not have the institutionalized processes for resolving internal conflict. Instead, top management concentrated on creating a "decision context" by the use

[18]Quoted in an unpublished, undated mimeo, "Strategy and Structure at ITT," INSEAD, France.

of temporary structures such as task forces and project teams complemented by the formal hierarchical structure. This practice carried over to the resolution of government issues. For example, in the major investment dispute between the North American and Latin American Divisions a special task force, under the powerful Corporate Strategy Staff, was created by top management. For issues requiring coordination *within* the International Automotive Operations its own Business Planning Staff performs a similar function; for intersubsidiary disputes within a region regional management serves as arbitrators.

Transfer of Experience

An important asset of the large multinational company is the ability to transfer knowledge and experience from one subsidiary to another. Though government issues vary considerably between regions and product sectors, certain fundamental commonalities exist across any international network as companies learn to survive and prosper in foreign environments.

MNC recognition and use of this "information asset" is a rather recent occurrence and its systematic exploitation even more so. An important manifestation of their increasing concern in this area has been the growth and development of the government-affairs function at both country and corporate levels. Given their full-time role of monitoring international negotiations and intergovernmental agreements, these government-affairs staffs have become a veritable store of valuable information on how the different parts of the company respond to or have been affected by government issues.

IBM is one company that makes a particular effort to exploit this resource. By allowing area external-affairs staffs to have access to business plans and country management reports it has greatly enhanced their role and effectiveness as advisors to country and company management. At the same time IBM has instituted a series of annual week-long conferences between external-affairs specialists from all corporate levels. The development of this global perspective has proved especially useful at the quarterly meetings between country managers in which considerable time is devoted to the discussion of government issues.

At Lilly the intercorporate transfer of experience tends to be much more structured along functional lines. For example, local product registration specialists in countries in which a new product has just been introduced hold special seminars for their counterpart specialists in other countries.

Though specific recognition and systematic use of corporate experience are of rather recent vintage, the very existence of a government-relations policy framework in these companies is an indication of their ability to incorporate a wide range of company experience into a consistent international strategy. Many of IBM's international government-relations policies, for example, evolved out of the deliberations of a 1967 task force of general managers formed in response to company concern with rising economic nationalism in Europe.

In all companies in the Assertive Mode the emphasis on government-relations management was consistency of response and outcome across issues and circumstances. This was primarily achieved by companywide adherence to a specific set of policy guidelines and facilitated by the design of decision contexts in which the issues could be quickly and predictably resolved. However, unlike the specific mechanism of conflict resolution or budgeting and planning, the process of experience and knowledge exchange in these Assertive companies has amounted to little more than a modest attempt at being informed. This was perhaps because of the greater control they exerted over the negotiations process than, say, those companies in the Structured Mode. Their higher degree of bargaining power vis-à-vis host governments, combined with the generally greater variety of their markets and products, leads to a high degree of fluidity across issues and circumstances: issues might resemble each other and call for identical solutions, but few issues require—as in the case of the Structured Mode companies—an identical team of issue-specific troubleshooters across countries and regions.

Corporate Culture

Implicit in all these company-specific procedures and mechanisms is an expression of the firm's individual corporate culture or the particular way it goes about managing its business. The very fact that all companies do things differently is not only a reflection of the difference between industries and strategies, but also of their own idiosyncratic approaches to their environment, honed and developed over the life of the company's experience.

For companies in the Assertive Mode the cultivation of this "corporate culture" is a particularly conscious and deliberate process. This is especially evident in the development of individual career paths and reward systems.

At both ITT and IBM career paths were national in scope, yet retained a distinct emphasis on the development of multiple perspectives. National managers were almost always local citizens and the companies fostered loyalty by granting long-tenured positions at the country level. Managers seldom moved horizontally between subsidiaries but vertically from national subsidiaries to corporate or area headquarters and then back to the original subsidiary, usually in a higher position. At IBM this grooming of management potential and loyalty was an individualized process that involved the development of close informal links between peers and the continual socialization of managers in the internal value systems of the company, where as at ITT it was a much more collective process in which management loyalty was cemented by a continual process of group decision making, peer review, and individual accountability.[19]

---

[19]In 1986 ITT, as part of a major strategic realignment of its businesses, sold its worldwide telecommunications operations to a consortium led by France's state-owned Compagnie Générale d'Électricité.

Establishing a sense of corporate value and identity can be developed only by extensive people-oriented efforts over long periods of time. By designing career paths that provide multiple perspectives companies such as IBM and Lilly seek to ensure that managers will be able to "see" issues from more than their current job-related perspective and to evaluate them on the basis of overall corporate interests. Further, by fostering a common value system the company encourages the development of a network of informal personal relationships and communications channels. These informal systems provide for a flexible management approach that facilitates effective management of government issues. Managers are encouraged to initiate cooperative interaction on major issues where multiple perspectives are needed. When such an environment prevails, issues can be tackled early in their life cycles and joint problem solving is facilitated.

Lilly epitomizes a company with a value-laden environment. The values frequently emphasized within the company include openness, honesty, and the need for mutual trust. These values tend to foster a highly cooperative corporate environment. Managers were provided with line and staff experience and frequently transferred from the area to functional or product responsibility. Each manager is evaluated not only by his line superiors but also by managers in other parts of the company with whom he has regular working relations. The effect of such intensive acculturalization into company values and broad exposure to a variety of perspectives and individuals tends to foster an overall decision-making environment that encourages cooperation and mutual accommodation on many issues that might otherwise result in conflict or require arbitration by a higher level.

3

The Diffuse Mode

DIFFUSE MODE DEFINED

Companies in the Diffuse Mode perceive the government issues as being external to regular corporate concerns; they wait for issues to arise, and then deal with them on a case-by-case basis. They generally have no specific government-relations strategies and their internal processes for treating individual issues as and when they form is characteristically varied: issues are either quickly propelled upward for resolution or stuck at the subunit level where linkage effects or overall corporate interests may not be adequately taken into account. Finally, companies in this mode evidence a notable lack of structural mechanisms and procedures for systematically articulating, analyzing, and responding to government issues.

The general response patterns of these companies bear a strong correspondence to the pure-type, Ad Hoc Approach described in Chapter 1: both deal with government issues only *after* they occur, and the decision process typically emphasizes short-run responses to short-run feedback, with no effort to categorize issue-areas systematically or incorporate them into long-run strategic planning systems. The general stance of companies in this mode is typically a reactive one. They not infrequently find themselves formulating responses under pressure —with the implication that issues can just as easily overwhelm as be resolved. In this respect the Diffuse Mode can also be viewed as a "firefighter's" approach to government-relations management.

This approach to government issues stands in marked contrast to the proactive, anticipatory approach of the Assertive Mode described in Chapter 2 and the Structured Mode in the following. In both cases host-country interests and concerns are viewed as an integral part of the overseas operations; and strategy, process, and structure all reflect considerable effort at the systematic recognition and resolution of government issues.

Two companies in this study fell into the Diffuse Mode: Cummins in diesel engine manufacturing and International Harvester in the heavy equipment manufacturing industry.[1]

---

[1]This chapter is based on experiences of these companies prior to 1982, when the primary research for this book was carried out. Since then the fates of Cummins and International Harvester have diverged significantly. Cummins went through a few tough years in the early 1980s because of a downturn in the U.S. and worldwide truck and industrial markets for which it supplied diesel engines, components, and replacement parts. In 1985 the company's markets were continuing their recovery and Cummins' sales were some 20% higher than in 1980. Internationally, Cummins expanded its operations with a licensing arrangement in Korea (1982), a major licensing agreement with China National Technical Import Corporation which covers several engine types (operational since 1982) and the establishment of Cummins Technical Service Center in the PRC, and in 1985 entered into two new licensing agreements—in Turkey with BMC Sanayi, a truck manufacturer, for the local production of engines and in Indonesia with Boma Bisma Indra, a government agency for the production of multiapplication engines. International Harvester, on the other hand, because of major financial difficulties, was forced to undertake a series of major restructurings of its businesses. In 1982 the company shed its construction equipment business and in 1985 sold off its agricultural equipment business. Today, it competes in North America as a manufacturer of medium- and heavy-duty diesel trucks under its new name, Navistar International Corporation.

Generally, companies displaying a diffuse approach to government-relations management are those for whom government issues have been historically of little importance. In order to have avoided government issues companies like Cummins and International Harvester in the Diffuse Mode evidence certain common characteristics: first, they are primarily situated in low profile, nonsalient industries that have traditionally offered no particular technological or market attraction to national governments. Further, these companies have the major bulk of their operations in the liberal economies of Europe in which specific government involvement is minimal. Their international strategies do not involve a high degree of interdependence among different country subsidiaries. Finally, their international spread is relatively narrow. Cummins was a relative newcomer to the international scene, whereas Harvester, after retrenchment from Latin America over the last few years, had major facilities in some eight countries. The size and scale of their country operations are typically small—both in terms of national profile and company sales volume.

CHARACTERISTICS OF COMPANIES: CHALLENGES FOR GOVERNMENT-RELATIONS MANAGEMENT

The lack of industry salience, absence of company strategies that emphasize an integrated network, and a narrow international spread all affect the level of company attention to government issues and their management of same.

Influence of Salience

Cummins is an independent manufacturer of diesel engines whose primary focus is the original equipment manufacturers' market of U.S.-based multinationals. International Harvester prior to 1982, was a major producer of three heavy equipment lines: trucks, agricultural equipment, and construction equipment.

Neither company attracts much government attention. Both represent mature industries with relatively low rates of technological innovation;[2] and although both are capital-intensive and scale economy-oriented neither comes close to the size and scale of the automobile industry or, for that matter, many other large, capital-intensive industries. For example, the minimum scale for an efficient tractor plant is only 5000 units per year.

The concentration of the major overseas operations of both companies in Europe means that they experienced little or no industry-specific regulation. For example, Cummins, in discussing its 1980 U.K. operations, emphasized that the nature of the company's major concern in the field of government relations was, in fact, with the *general macroeconomic* policies of the government:

> Profits in 1979 would have been better except for our results in the U.K. . . . With the government pursuing an aggressive and controversial program to reduce inflation and restore competitive performance . . . there has been a deep contraction in the manufacturing sector of the U.K. economy without benefit of a similar decline in inflation. At the same time, the economic policies . . . have resulted in increasing the value of the pound . . . exports have shrunk dramatically.

> Since this problem began in 1979, we have made a series of adjustments in an effort to reduce the impact of these U.K. government policy decisions on Cummins. These include: special marketing programs, vigorous cost and working capital controls, and pricing actions. Because of the severity and extended duration of the problem, we have also made structural changes to moderate

[2]By 1984 Cummins' Annual Report listed a number of initiatives that involved technological developments: work on ceramic materials for diesel engine components, new manufacturing and process technologies, and the formation of Cummins Venture Corporation to invest directly in new technologies. Although the pace of technological development was accelerating, diesel engines were, and are, not seen as leading-edge, high-technology products.

these effects. We have sourced materials as rapidly as possible to take advantage of the relationship of sterling to other currencies.[3]

In Latin America the role of government was different for both companies. There Cummins and Harvester were faced with the usual government demands placed on multinationals. These centered on the levels of local value-added and exports, ownership requirements, and so on. But Latin American operations were of only marginal significance to both companies until 1976. It is noteworthy that Harvester, which once had substantial operations in Latin America in the 1960s, had gradually pulled out of Brazil, Peru, and Argentina, partly in response to constant government demands and interference.

Because neither Cummins nor Harvester was particularly pressured by government concerns up until the late 1970s, they could therefore afford to manage government issues on a diffuse basis. The situation changed dramatically as both companies began to move into Latin America in the mid-1970s and were forced to contend with a greater degree of government intervention in their operations.

Influence of Company Strategy

Though both Cummins and International Harvester had been overseas for a number of years (Harvester, in fact, boasted of having sold its first tractor overseas in the last century), in terms of international strategy and organizational structure both were still in the early stages of overseas expansion. Both were essentially domestically oriented "international companies" rather than true multinational corporations: Cummins had not ventured much beyond the United States and United Kingdom and Harvester's rather extensive overseas operations were orga-

[3]Cummins Engine Company, *Annual Report*, 1980.

nized in a loose "federal" structure with considerable autonomy granted to the individual country subsidiary. Neither of these strategies was especially vulnerable to or affected by specific government pressures or demands.

Cummins' overall corporate strategy was based on the company's declared objective of maintaining its market leadership in cost-effective and fuel-efficient diesel engines. In keeping with this strategy, the company had concentrated its overseas manufacturing operations in the United Kingdom, where it had six plants, and France, where it had one components-manufacturing facility. The United States and United Kingdom served as primary export bases for markets in other parts of the world (74% of U.K. production was for export), and prior to 1975 the company had two license and joint-venture manufacturing facilities in India and Japan. With its major overseas operations concentrated in the relatively liberal economies of Europe, the combination of a marketing emphasis on original equipment manufacturers (OEMs) and the centralized sourcing patterns further diminished the potential for being confronted with significant government demands affecting their operations.

This relatively simple and focused corporate strategy was reflected in the company's centralized organizational structure and the delegation of all manufacturing responsibilities—both domestic and international—to corporate manufacturing staff. The company had an International Division organized along geographic lines, which was responsible for worldwide marketing.

International Harvester, on the other hand, appeared to have no consistent overall company strategy and its organizational structure reflected this condition. With manufacturing operations in France, Germany, the United Kingdom, Canada, and Australia, Harvester's international structure could best be described as a loose federal system in which country subsidiaries were profit centers and country managers were individually responsible for all three product lines. Though the Overseas Division had established regional offices to oversee and control subsidiary operations, product and functional staffs were primarily country support-oriented and headquarters intervention was both limited and infrequent. Even decisions of company-wide importance were frequently made on the largely unchallenged recommendations of country managers.

It should be emphasized that this country-oriented structure developed more by default than design: unlike ITT, Harvester had no particular government pressure to keep it in this particular mold.

The result was a staggering proliferation of product designs and parts as each country manager geared his operations to meet his own local priorities. For example, at one point its eight plants were manufacturing a total of 57 different engine design models and multiple product development programs continued to turn out more. Whereas this permitted Harvester to adapt to different market segments in different countries, it also resulted in a confusing situation of inconsistent sourcing patterns and manufacturing duplications that represented substantial cost penalties.

Finally, in 1977, under extreme pressure to rationalize its international operations, Harvester reorganized into four worldwide product groups, each with its own mandate: Truck, Agricultural Equipment, Construction Equipment, and Component Parts. Agriculture and Trucks were organized geographically into three regions: North America, Europe-Middle East-Africa, and Asia-Pacific; whereas the Construction Equipment Group organized along worldwide functional lines. The Component Parts Group was made into an internal profit center whose prices were required to be competitive with outside suppliers.

Within three years this restructuring effort had succeeded in reducing the number of engine models from 57 to 30 (with the eventual target of 15) and a new truck line was introduced that required 30% fewer parts. However, the combination of the structural adjustments and the addition of new top-management talent recruited from outside the company also led to substantial power shifts within the International Division as the influence of country managers declined in favor of the new divisional product and functional staff. Government issues, which had once been localized and managed by country managers, now had to be dealt with within the more complex and multiple lines of communication of the new product division structure by area and division management.

Neither strategy—Cummins' centralized manufacturing or Harvester's federalism—implied a significant penalty from diffuse mode of government-relations management. This sharply contrasts with the situation facing companies that pursue a strategy of integration, such as IBM and Ford, where penalties from inconsistent or disjointed incremental responses to government issues were potentially high.

Influence of Spread

Though International Harvester boasted of a much longer history of overseas involvement than Cummins, both companies, with international sales averaging less than one-third of the total operations, were still only moderately multinational. They were also among the smallest firms in our sample, with sales of only $1.96 billion for Cummins and $7 billion for Harvester. At the same time the overwhelming majority of their sales and operations were in the "Anglo-Saxon commonwealth" or Europe, where governments paid them relatively little attention.

As we have already discussed, the public policy climates confronting these companies differed substantially between Europe and Latin America. As such, they faced few common issues between regions that required similar responses. Thus there was little incentive to develop or codify internal policies on issues. Nor was there much need to develop mechanisms to transfer knowledge and experience between regions.

GOVERNMENT-RELATIONS STRATEGY

Companies in the Diffuse Mode are characterized by a general lack of consistent, overall government-relations strategies. Government issues are dealt with in a piecemeal, ad hoc manner, with emphasis on short-run answers to short-run problems. Moreover, unlike Assertive or Structured companies, there are no centralized government-relations policies or guidelines, systematic response patterns, or extrastructural mechanisms for the facilitation of government-issue resolution. To the extent that these companies do have a government-relations strategy it can best be described as "deal with governments only when you have to."

This absence of a strategic focus on government issues is directly reflected in the relatively low-key position of government-relations management in their overall strategic and operational decision making. Government issues historically have had little impact on their operations; and the costs of keeping them low on the priority list have been viewed traditionally as less than the costs of specifically organizing to deal with them.

An important distinction to note, however, is that the companies included here tend to be reactive, which is not necessarily the same as an Ad Hoc Approach. Whereas Assertive companies may choose to respond in an ad hoc manner, a Reactive Approach implies response under pressure. Assertive companies anticipate government actions and have a wide range of well developed response patterns from which to choose—including ad hoc responses—whereas Diffuse companies confront each issue as, and when, it develops. Thus, when important issues do appear, the response of companies in the Diffuse Mode is sometimes more akin to crisis management and "firefighting" than systematic, rational issue resolution.

The dynamics of this are easy to see: lack of strategy fosters a

lack of systematic response, which fosters organizational iner-
tia, whereas the lack of familiarity with government issues fosters an inability to discriminate between them and to assess
adequately their impact on the firm.

The costs of being reactive in government-relations management are obvious; they are also cumulative and negatively rein-
forcing, for the failure to respond adequately in a timely fashion
in one case may set the stage for more drastic adjustments later
if the government persists and escalates its demands. In such
situations the costs of internal adjustments to accommodate
government concerns may rise commensurately: the longer a
necessary change is put off, the harder it is to implement and
the more complicated its implications for the overall management of the firm. Further, inconsistent responses take their inevitable toll over time.

Yet even companies that are diffuse demonstrate a general
tendency to develop more consistent strategies and response
patterns if only to keep government-relations management
within a comfortable range of neglect. The problem in recent
years, however, has been the pace of these incremental adjustments which, in general, has not kept up with the pace of governmental change and the growing international dialogue on
the place of multinational companies in the world economy.

In recent years this situation has tended to force many Diffuse companies into an eventual day of reckoning. The whole
process of change and adjustment to government issues is telescoped into an intense period of company-wide reassessment
and reorganization. This process is usually triggered by the surfacing of a significant government issue, or series of issues, the
implications of which, for the firm, are important enough to
propel management into awareness, commitment, and action.

Until the mid-1970s both Cummins and International Harvester could have been considered archetypical Diffuse companies. As discussed, neither had a consistent, overall government-relations strategy nor any significant policy or structural

framework for the management of government issues. (To be sure, International Harvester did not even appear to have a consistent, overall *operational* strategy.) It is also true, however, that until the mid-1970s the management of government relations was not high on their list of priorities.

The most significant example of the lack of strategic focus was the organization of International Harvester's fairly extensive overseas operations into a loose federal structure in which the major strategic and operating powers were in the hands of the individual country managers. The economic contradictions of this type of management structure—in the form of product duplication, multiple development efforts, and inconsistent sourcing patterns—were at one point estimated to represent an excess of $600 million in operating costs.[4] Thus the first organizational restructuring of overseas operations (1977) was in response to economic pressures and the lack of an overall operational strategy rather than the need to develop a specific government-relations strategy.

It is interesting to note in this regard that despite this massive reorganization Harvester's dealings with host governments were just as inconsistent and unfocused *after* the changes occurred as before. For example, the same company that had pulled out of Latin America some years ago as a reaction to intolerable government interference in its business was the first to agree to Mexico's restrictive investment terms—terms at which all the other competing companies balked. That this inconsistency in strategic focus was matched by inconsistency in the process of dealing with government issues was also noticeably apparent after the reorganization as the new product division managers began to take up their mandates. Whereas one division completely bypassed local managers in a significant investment decision, in another division the responsibility for negotiating with government officials was left entirely to the local joint-

[4]E.T. Christiansen, International Harvester (B), ICCH Case 4-381-053, 1980.

venture partners. At the same time the involvement of corporate top management was highly sporadic and interdivisional coordination remained minimal at best.

Cummins, on the other hand, was a company with a definite, clear-cut strategy (to produce low-cost, fuel-efficient engines and to maintain leadership in the OEM market). Their problem was therefore not so much the lack of strategic focus as the primacy of operational imperatives over government-relations concerns. All Cummins corporate policy and decision making was based on strict economic logic, with little acknowledgment of the noneconomic imperatives. Although there was an appreciation of the political requirements of dealing with governments overseas, the company was not comfortable in assessing or handling government-relations issues. This was clearly demonstrated in the company's initially slow reaction to Brazilian government demands for more value-added in their newly formed joint venture in that country and in their initially slow refusal to enter into a joint-venture arrangement with their Mexican state-owned licensing partners. In part, the slowness was deliberate as the company tried to sort out the risks on a case-by-case basis. Cummins had always felt that it was a capital-short company with more opportunities than resources. As a result it had to balance its desire to grow and exercise market leadership overseas with its felt lack of resources and experience. Thus Cummins' diffuse government-relations strategy should be viewed as the natural consequence of an existing international strategy.

GOVERNMENT-RELATIONS PROCESS

The lack of overall government-relations strategies is clearly reflected in the way in which Diffuse companies manage government issues in terms of internal corporate-response processes and external company-government interface. Predictably, there are no significant patterns in these processes—just as there are no government-relations policies or structural mechanisms—and issues are generally dealt with in a relatively ad hoc manner. The key variable in how an issue is managed tends to be its origin, not its importance to overall company interests, because importance may be only marginally (or subsequently) discerned.

In keeping with the lack of strategic focus in this mode, most government issues are handled within the regular structure of the firm; and, unlike Assertive or Structured response patterns, there is little or no recourse to extrastructural mechanisms or procedures for the facilitation of the interdivisional coordination on issues with a broader reach. As with most companies, senior corporate management in the Diffuse Mode is typically responsible for only the most visible and important issues, such as investment and ownership decisions; however, given the lack of clear-cut policies and response patterns in the companies they manage, they often find themselves embroiled in local issues of little companywide concern. Finally, the development of a specific government-affairs function is limited at best and in no case involves any significant allocation of company resources or talent.

This lack of consistent, overall government-relations strategies finds reflection in the highly eclectic, internal-response processes of International Harvester. As noted in the preceding section, prior to 1977 Harvester's country managers were lords over their own fiefdoms. Even though the formal structure of the corporation provided for an International Division and a Worldwide Export Marketing subsidiary, in the absence of specific company policies or guidelines—and given the relatively placid nature of economic and political relations with host governments—most of strategic and operation decision-making power devolved to the individual subsidiary manager.

With the formation of three worldwide product divisions in 1977, the general locus of decision-making power moved up the

corporate ladder to the divisional level; at the same time, however, each new product division was allowed to develop its
own separate mandate on all operational and strategic issues.
Thus, despite the wider, overall corporate perspective this new
structure provided, the management of government issues and
government relations remained highly fragmented and inconsistent both within and between the divisional units. In their concern for overall economic rationalization and product efficiency
little attention had been paid to the systematic formulation of
company policies and guidelines on government-relations management.

For example, shortly after the general corporate reorganization the Construction Equipment (CE) Group initiated two separate negotiations procedures for major new investment proposals in countries in which it already had significant operations:
one in Mexico for the establishment of a $22-million, joint-
venture project and the other in Canada for the addition of two
new rubber loaders to their Canadian product line in return for
the duty-free import into Canada of crawlers and heavy-duty
loaders. The latter was part of a general rationalization program
to bring Canadian operations more in line with those of the
United States.

In the first case, which involved negotiations with the Mexican government, CE division management completely bypassed
the existing country managers and placed its top executives
directly in charge of the detailed bargaining over balance of
payments, local value-added requirements, and so on. In the
Canadian case, however, though the proposal itself emanated
from division management, all government negotiations were
left entirely to the local country managers.

At the same time Harvester's Agricultural Equipment (AE)
Group demonstrated yet another variation on this theme by allowing its Brazilian joint-venture partners (country nationals) to
handle all government issues with only minimal supervision
from division management. The CE Group followed this partic-

ular lead in its search for a Nigerian joint-venture partner with "sufficient influence." Like their pre-1977 reliance on local expertise, product division management in the reorganized corporate structure appeared to depend heavily on local advice and opinion.

This lack of a consistent, overall approach to government-relations management was also reflected in the absence of specific mechanisms and procedures for the coordination of issues *between* product divisions. Before the 1977 reorganization an informal consultation process between individual country managers served to coordinate issues between areas and product groups. After the reorganization no intercorporate mechanisms were provided for: the division of company operations into three worldwide product divisions created a situation of multiple country managers at the national level, each responsible for a specific product line and reporting exclusively to that division. Recognizing the importance of maintaining a semblance of company integrity at the national level, Harvester designated the largest group subsidiary manager as "Mr. International Harvester" for the entire country, responsible for all company-government relations. This was essentially the only structural concession to government-relations management introduced at the time. In the absence of lateral coordinating procedures between divisions, many country and product division managers at headquarters objected to having another division manager represent their interests. For example, in one instance the management of the Australian subsidiary of the Truck Group refused to have the designated senior country manager—in this case the head of the AE Group—represent their interests in an investment negotiation with the Australian government.

This lack of interdivisional coordination became painfully apparent in a mid-1970s situation that found two separate Harvester groups negotiating at the same time with the Algerian government, each unaware, or unmindful, of the other's proceedings. The CE Group was negotiating with the state-owned

enterprise Sonocom for the turnkey sale of a crawler tractor
plant while the Truck Group was discussing the sale of $10 mil-
lion worth of International Harvester trucks to Sonatrach, the
national oil company. When the Algerians insisted on a complete training and performance guarantee as a condition for
securing the Sonocom deal, CE withdrew without considering
the impact of its refusal on the Truck Group negotiations. Natu-
rally the latter wound up with egg on their faces and the whole
Algerian episode ended in failure.

In the absence of extrastructural mechanisms for the lateral
coordination of issues between divisions, corporate top management was the only group that could see fast and far enough
into both the adverse and the beneficial impact of individual
decisions on different subunits within the company. The ability
to incorporate this wider perspective into the decision-making
process was clearly demonstrated in the negotiations between
International Harvester and the Spanish government for a joint
trucking venture in the Spanish market.

In anticipation of the 1983 accession to the EEC, the Spanish
government had developed specific plans to modernize its old,
inefficient trucking industry and in 1980 sent a special com-
mercial delegation to the United States to seek out a new joint-
venture partner with suitable technology and capital. Because
the Truck Group of International Harvester was the least international of the three divisions, the delegation made its first con-
tacts directly with senior corporate management in Chicago.
Perceiving an opportunity to gain a low-cost toehold in the
Common Market, corporate management endorsed the Spanish
proposal and established a project team consisting primarily of
functional staff from the Truck Group to draw up the plans.
Overall responsibility for the negotiations, however, was not
vested in the Truck Group but rather in the hands of James
Doyle, then a ranking member of corporate top management
who, from his lofty corporate perch, also began to see Spanish
opportunities for Harvester's Agricultural Group and was to tie

the two issues together to get around Spain's highly protected agricultural equipment market. Following the successful landing of the truck deal in 1981, Doyle also managed to secure government permission to import, assemble, and eventually manufacture Harvester AE products in Spain. This was the first time corporate management had systematically considered the intergroup opportunities in an investment-decision negotiation.

Although top management is able to incorporate a wider perspective, it should be pointed out that in this case the initiation of the issue directly with the top management of the firm was fortuitous. Had the initial contact or subsequent dealings been with the Truck Group management, it is not clear that the interests of other product divisions would have been taken into account. Thus for top management to provide a cross-product division perspective an issue must rise to them, but this assumes that the middle managers within a product division at the frontline of dealing with issues will be able to evaluate and discern when a particular issue has broader implications and raise it upward in the organizational hierarchy: often this is unlikely to be the case.

In companies that lack procedural form or structure for the resolution of government issues the treatment an issue does get is largely subject to idiosyncratic factors, the most significant of which are the personality and character of the manager on the front line. For example, a strong frontline manager may succeed in predetermining the outcome of an issue by the way he handles it: on the one hand, he may feel qualified to make the decision himself; on the other hand, even when he lacks the requisite authority, in the absence of a codified set of company policies and guidelines he may bias the definition of the issue in a way that will achieve his preferred outcomes. The danger is that, while addressing the immediate problem and facilitating the job of higher management levels, the lack of an overall company perspective on the issue may commit the company to a course of action that might in the long run be suboptimal. At the same time the frequent resolution of important issues at lower levels of management can easily lead to the *inconsistency* of response across subunits and issue areas. This not only costs the company in terms of lost "economies of learning" but, if the responses are inconsistent enough, it also tends to damage the credibility of the company in the government's eyes.

A clear example of the influence of frontline managers on the internal corporate process can be seen in the experience of Cummins' Latin American Marketing Staff over the question of company investment in the Andean Pact countries. In 1976 the newly formed pact began to solicit bids for the establishment of five new diesel engine plants throughout the region (Decision 120). The Latin American Marketing manager at the time was aware of this development but, in keeping with the company's conservative posture and general lack of familiarity with the area, expressed no particular interest in submitting a bid. In 1978, however, when a new manager took his place, the company reacted in a very different manner. Perceiving, in the new common market, an opportunity to create a regional integrated manufacturing network, the new manager adopted the issue as his own personal project and, together with a full-time staff aide and another senior corporate executive (who had developed a special affinity for the project), spent several months in and out of Bogota lobbying for and finally securing the last of the five plant assignments (the others already having been captured by competitors).

The front-line managers had substituted their initiative and vision in the absence of an overall corporate policy in this area. In this particular instance the strategic rationale for the initiatives of those involved is not difficult to discern. Cummins, they felt, could not afford not to be a player in the Andean Pact, should it materialize—especially given the initiatives of major competitors. To do nothing might well mean finding Cummins locked out by tariff barriers. As it turned out the Andean Pact projects never materialized. After Chile pulled out of the pact and a change in government called Peru's commitment into question the other investors hesitated. This provoked an impatient Venezuela into cancelling all its original bids and calling for new ones. By this time the new manager had been transferred and the International Division had acquired a new head who, confident of his recent Latin American initiatives, offered two new bids to the Venezuelan government.

At the time the Andean affair was unfolding the head of Cummins' International Marketing Division was also negotiating with a newly formed Third World common market, the ASEAN treaty nations, for the establishment of an assembly plant in Singapore. Here, too, the motivation was analogous to the Andean Pact initiative, and in 1981 the company was forced to admit that this project had also been shelved, "pending resolution of the ASEAN common market's discussions."

In situations in which the frontline manager has a less forceful personality with no inclination to substitute his own vision for company policy government issues can easily be passed up the corporate ladder to higher and wider perspectives, which, at least in theory, should better guarantee the corporate interest. In the absence of specific policies and guidelines, however, the danger at this level is more likely to be the lack of sufficient knowledge of an issue or awareness of its importance in the local context. Thus the resolution of a government issue may be suboptimal and may commit the company to a less-than-desirable course of action. At the same time this "leveling up" of issues in the absence of an adequate policy, or structure to deal with them, also tends to result in an overload on top management's time and talent—the result being that issues tend to languish and go unresolved. In this case the response process becomes one of nonresponse, as typified by managerial comments such as, "Let's wait and see," "We don't know if the government is serious," or "Maybe it will just disappear." The risk, of course, is that the government may get increasingly annoyed and act unilaterally.

For many companies in the Diffuse Mode, therefore, the substantive response to an issue begins only after the government bares its stick. It is only when the distant caretaker turns into a nosey landlord, objecting to one's life-style and threatening to raise one's rent, that the seriousness of an issue becomes apparent and specific courses of action begin to surface. Decision makers are better able to calculate the specific costs of ignoring government demands versus the specific costs of organizing to deal with them. How much internal harmony must the firm forego to accommodate the local politicians?

Thus an Ad Hoc Approach to the management of government issues can quickly take on a decidedly reactive cast. The time involved in bringing an issue to the attention of the appropriate corporate powers, combined with the time it takes to obtain sufficient information and adequately evaluate a response, may seriously hamper a company's ability to respond in a timely and efficient manner to issues of government concern. This may politicize or escalate an issue, harden the government's position, and lead to less than optimal solutions or compromises. Ex post facto, it is difficult to evaluate whether or not the realized outcomes are indeed inferior to the outcomes that could have resulted at an earlier stage in the issue's company-government life cycle; however, the sum of this inconsistent and equivocating response to government issues invariably results in a less-than-optimal company-government relationship and may hasten the necessity for a significant day of reckoning.

The implications of a Diffuse company posture is clearly illustrated in the sequence of events that surrounded Cummins' first moves into the Latin American market. In 1975 the company established a small joint venture in Brazil which initiated a series of company headaches over the incessant government demands for compliance with a continually changing set of economic and industry regulations. But, when, in 1978, it presented the company with an order to increase substantially all exports and local value-added in order to retain existing import licenses, the company balked and did nothing. Around the same time Cummins was approached by its license partner in Mexico, DINA, S.A. (a state-owned monopoly producer of light-duty diesel engines), with an offer to enter into a substantial joint-venture arrangement for the expansion of existing capacity and product lines.

In both cases the issues were referred to the Corporate Manufacturing Staff which had overall decision-making authority for all international operations. The Corporate Manufacturing staff studied the issues but in both cases demurred: neither case made sense from an economic point of view and both deviated from the overall strategic focus on market leadership in the low-cost, fuel-efficient diesel-engine market.

As the company pondered the merits and demerits of each case, the two governments grew increasingly impatient and began to pressure the company for a response. However, it was only after DINA turned its back and began negotiating with General Motors and the Brazilian government began to issue substantial threats that top management finally began to react.

At this point Michael Walsh, who had recently been recruited to join the ranks of senior management at Cummins, was given the assignment of heading the International Marketing Division, thus assuming responsibility for both Latin American projects. This was a clear signal that significant change was in the offing. Within a year, with the active participation of the Chairman, Henry Schacht, and the Chief Financial Officer, Walsh had negotiated two agreements that differed substantially from previous corporate policy. In Brazil he agreed to a five-year, $60-million export commitment for the existing joint venture. In addition, Cummins bought out the 51% ownership interest of its Brazilian partner and in July 1981 Cummins Brasil S.A. began operations as a wholly owned subsidiary. In

Mexico he agreed to a $41-million investment that represented Cummins' 40% equity in a new joint-venture project with DINA for the manufacture of a wide range of engines to begin operations in 1982. The latter was of special significance to the company for three reasons: first of all it transformed a passive licensing relationship into the largest company investment outside the United Kingdom and Canada; second it opened the Mexican market to other Cummins' products in exchange for a balanced trade commitment; and third, along with the now wholly owned Brazilian operations, it represented a significant strategic commitment to the Latin American market and to a substantial departure from overall company strategy. Top management had realized that international operations could not be evaluated strictly on economic grounds; that other factors such as competitors' moves, the establishment of a strategic foothold, and future unquantifiable government relations benefits were equally, if not more, important.

GOVERNMENT-RELATIONS STRUCTURE

The formal structure of a company in the Diffuse Mode is not geared in any significant way to the management of government relations. Government issues are dealt with almost exclusively *within* the regular structure of the firm, and the nature of company response patterns is generally dependent on the particular personalities of the line and staff people on the front line. Unlike Structured or Assertive companies, there is little or no recourse made to the use of extrastructural mechanisms for interdivisional coordination; and the development of a specific government-affairs function is embryonic at best.

In the absence of a set of corporate policies or recognized precedents for dealing with government issues decision making in a Diffuse company tends to reflect a disproportionate use of top-management resources and talent. The substantive decision-making role on major investment and ownership issues is not surprising; what is surprising, however, is the seeming necessity for their involvement in the particulars of local issues and interdivisional squabbles.

Both Cummins and International Harvester were archetypical Diffuse companies prior to the mid-1970s. It is significant to note that each underwent substantial structural change as it moved into the Latin American market where the public policy climate forced it to take greater account of the influence of host governments over company affairs.

Cummins' experience in Latin America represents a classical example of the corporate learning process and the successive states through which a company moves from a purely domestic producer to a bona fide multinational corporation: in elegant sequence Cummins had moved through the 1960s and 1970s from exporting to licensing, to European-based manufacturing and exporting, to worldwide manufacturing; and at each point its organizational structure followed shortly behind.

As a result of the problems in Mexico and Brazil, Cummins' management realized that the worldwide functional structure, which had served them so well in the United Kingdom, was no longer adequate for their new operations in Latin America. The International Marketing Staff, with their geography-oriented perspective, understood the need to adapt to government conditions, whereas the globally-oriented International Manufacturing Staff was much more concerned with maintaining the company's competitive position. Although Corporate Manufacturing had formal decision-making power in both cases, the International Marketing Staff held their ground and forced the issue up to the corporate level for resolution, where it rested for several weeks as senior managers attempted to catch up with the specifics. These cases involved not only a conflict of perspective between the two functional groups but also, as it was beginning to dawn on them, a significant misfit of corporate strategy and structure in the management of their new international operations.

It was only after Mexico initiated talks with General Motors and the Brazilian government began to threaten sanctions that the company agreed to turn the whole situation over to the geographic expertise of the International Marketing Staff. At the same time top management appointed Michael Walsh, a member of senior management, to preside over the changes and to negotiate with the host governments. When the two agreements were finally signed, the Manufacturing Staff was directed to adjust its sourcing patterns and manufacturing operations accordingly.

In the process of negotiating these two new agreements with the Mexican and Brazilian governments, Walsh was able to demonstrate to corporate management that the management of joint ventures and licensing arrangements had little in common with the management of wholly owned subsidiaries in Europe and required a different organizational structure to accommodate them. As a result top management decided to create a new staff function to handle all nonwholly owned operations, reporting to Walsh, who continued to head the International Marketing Division.

In addition to this new staff group Cummins instituted a system of monthly meetings between corporate executives and functional staffs to consider companywide sourcing and resource allocation decisions—primarily for the benefit of the displaced Manufacturing Staff. In 1981 Cummins had not yet defined the boundaries of its new international strategy. In the words of one senior manager at the time:

> We have these meetings, but we do not have a multiplant sourcing strategy . . . unlike some competitors, we do not have a component interchange system. We have come a long way in understanding that meeting government concerns are an integral

part of the marketing mix in Latin America, but we still have some ways to go. . . .[5]

By 1985, however, Cummins had indeed come a long way. Cummins' international network had expanded to include major licensing arrangements in South Korea, China, Turkey, and Indonesia to complement its already substantial operations in Brazil, the joint venture in Mexico, and a 20-year-old joint venture in India. Cummins' international strategy recognized the need to have local operations to serve these large developing country markets, which it considered "closed" to exports.[6] But beyond this the company was actively examining the potential of these operations as sourcing points or bases for serving other country markets. As stated explicitly in its 1984 Annual Report:

> In these . . . countries, we continue to look for ways to broaden our markets and to utilize our manufacturing bases as low-cost sources of components and purchased material for plants in other areas.

International Harvester, on the other hand, was an example of a company that didn't learn until it was too late. In the words of one consultant who examined the company in the early 1970s:

> . . . the environment of International Harvester is staid, old-fashioned, conservative, inbred, and non-entrepreneurial, an atmosphere of strict observance of protocol, status consciousness and stuffiness . . . decisions [are made] from a short-term perspective rather than weighted against long-term goals [and] there was no strategic planning or management systems to speak of.[7]

[5] Personal communication.
[6] See Cummins Engine Company, Inc., *Annual Report*, 1984.
[7] Mentioned in E.T. Christiansen, International Harvester (A), ICCH Case 4-381-052, 1980.

As late as 1976 one company executive characterized Harvester management style:

> ... the mushroom theory of decision-making - keep managers in the dark, and requests for resources will pop up all over the place, at random, and with no relation to each other. We had to think about the relations.[8]

In 1977 International Harvester reorganized itself for the second time in 34 years, going from its loose "federal" system to a tight, worldwide product division structure. The designers of this structure further permitted each product division to develop its own internal organizational structure, while vesting centralized control over three important areas to corporate staffs: engines and component parts manufacture, major investment and resource allocation decisions (vested in the hands of a new Planning Staff Group attached to corporate headquarters), and basic design and engineering complementarity across separate divisional product lines.

The only significant structural concession to the specific exigencies of government-relations management was the designation within each country of a senior country manager from among the three product divisions to handle all company–government affairs within the country. This usually fell to the country product manager of the largest divisional subsidiary.

The implications of this new structural reorganization for the management of government relations were threefold. To begin with, the role of the new senior country manager was not uniformly implemented. For example, in the United Kingdom, where both the Truck and AE Groups had long-established operations, no "senior country manager" was designated and each country product manager continued to deal directly with the government, whereas in France the AE Group manager succeeded in consolidating enough local power to represent the

---

[8]Christiansen, op. cit.

concerns of all three divisions at the national level. At the same time, in other cases in which the situation was less clear-cut, this new system tended to foster interdivisional conflict at both the country and regional levels; either one country product manager resisted the other's authority or, as in the case of the CE Group investment in Mexico, the divisional product manager often went over the heads of the local country managers to deal directly with national governments. In the latter case it will be recalled that the company already had significant AE and CE Group investments in Mexico and the authority of their respective managers had only recently been recast.

The second important implication of this new structure on the management of government relations concerned the multiplicity of management levels and functional staff that resulted. Whereas the previous structure had at least provided for informal coordination between country managers, in the new system the only formal coordination mechanism was the regular organizational hierarchy.

In this situation the resolution of government issues was largely dependent on the ability of middle managers to evaluate adequately the implications and properly refer their findings to the appropriate level of management. In the absence of overall corporate policies or systematic response processes this dependence on the middle managers gave rise to an inconsistency of response patterns across divisional lines and issue-areas, with some issues rising quickly to the top and others stopping at the frontline.

Third, in the absence of a formal, or informal, mechanism for intergroup coordination, it became increasingly difficult to learn from the mistakes of—or, for that matter, to capitalize on the goodwill created by—other product divisions in company-government negotiations. This resulted in the increasing involvement of senior-level corporate management in the details of entry-level negotiations, as clearly illustrated in James Doyle's handling of the Spanish trucking project.

In 1978 Harvester management created a separate Corporate Policy Committee consisting of senior corporate executives and product group presidents to address specifically the issues of interdivisional coordination. Previously, if one group had something to say to another, the message had to go all the way up one group ladder to the President and then all the way down the next for sufficient coordination to take place. Despite the improvement, however, the Corporate Policy Committee was the only structure to deal with the most important issues; senior management had neither the time nor the expertise to consider the more minor issues of cross-product coordination that developed farther down the corporate hierarchy.

In terms of structural context, neither Harvester nor Cummins had well developed administrative systems. Both had begun to experiment with strategic planning only in the late 1970s (having relied earlier on more informal control systems); but even in 1981, with formal planning, budgeting, and control systems in operation, there was little evidence of the systematic evaluation of government issues.

At the same time, there were no formal procedures for resolving conflicts or mechanisms for transferring knowledge that dealt specifically with government issues. This was in contrast to the specific systems that were developed and implemented in several of the Assertive companies, as described in Chapter 2.

A COMPANY IN TRANSITION

Xerox Corporation is an outstanding example of a company in transition from the Diffuse to the Assertive Mode of government-relations management. Three distinct phases were included in this transition. Prior to 1977 the company displayed a clearly Ad Hoc Approach to dealing with government issues. In late 1977, as a result of a series of government problems, especially in Latin America, top management initiated certain administrative changes "to institutionalize an awareness of the importance of external relations and to make appropriate action plans for dealing with changes in the external environment." In 1978 the new systems were implemented in the Latin American operating groups and in 1980 the systems were extended worldwide to Rank Xerox, Xerox Canada, and Fuji Xerox. During the same period, as Xerox began to diversify from its traditional reprographics business toward automated electronic office-equipment systems overseas, it ran headlong into a significantly more salient industry sector for which government-owned PTTs set technical standards, determined tariff schedules, and could bar foreign suppliers through purchasing policy. The challenge of government relations thus began to take on even more daunting proportions and called for significant structured and strategic adaptation.

Prior to 1977: A Reactor[9]

Xerox, the undisputed industry leader in the still rapidly growing photocopying market, had more than half the worldwide market share in 1977. Its overseas operations were coordinated by three operating groups: Xerox of Canada, Rank Xerox, and Xerox Latin America Group.

Xerox pursued a regional integrated strategy in its overseas operations. Manufacturing facilities in Europe, involving plants in Britain, Holland, France, and Spain, were managed by corporate manufacturing staffs based in the United States. Rank Xerox, a majority-owned joint venture based in London, managed a large network of marketing subsidiaries throughout Europe, Africa, the Middle-East, and Asia.

[9]For developments prior to 1977 and the initial introduction of the company's Issue Monitoring System, see Adam Meyerson, "International Relations at Xerox," Harvard Business School, ICCH case 9-380-159, 1980. I have drawn on material in the case for this period.

Xerox's major manufacturing operations in Latin America were in Brazil and Mexico and minor operations were scattered in several countries. These operations, too, were integrated and managed by functional manufacturing staff at the area level. Unlike Rank Xerox, the Xerox Latin America Group, based in Greenwich, Connecticut, oversaw all manufacturing as well as marketing operations which extended over 23 Latin American countries and 11 Caribbean islands. The operating group combined a regionwide functional organization with an area organization for operating line responsibilities. Functional staff at area headquarters made decisions on manufacturing, marketing, service, financial, and personnel issues. Operating vice presidents exercised line authority over the managing directors in country subsidiaries, and made sure that they implemented area headquarters' policies and met financial and other objectives. In these goals headquarters was aided by a formal, frequent, and heavily quantified reporting and evaluation system.

The copier industry was generally not considered a salient industry by governments. Like Cummins and Harvester, the public policy climate which Xerox faced in Europe was relatively free from sector or company-specific government intervention. In Latin America the story was different from Europe: like all other multinationals, Xerox was confronted with a variety of issues involving import restrictions, local value-added requirements, financial regulations, and so on. During the mid-1970s Xerox was surprised by a number of unwelcome government problems in Latin America that threatened its share of some markets.

In the mid-1970s two Xerox subsidiaries were advocating conflicting positions in the tariff reduction provisions of LAFTA's regional trade liberalization agreement. One national subsidiary, a net exporter within the region, was pressing for lower tariffs on copiers on the grounds that its revenues and earnings would shoot up considerably. The other subsidiary objected, however, for it was fearful that the local government, a net importer within the region, would be angry at any multinational urging tariff reduction; this subsidiary management feared that the local government might make import licenses harder to obtain and would perhaps withdraw from the trade liberalization agreement altogether. Dan Sharp, who as the Director of Inter-American Affairs was in charge of the coordinating company position with respect to LAFTA talks, had to decide between these positions. Even though not pressing for lower tariffs would, in the short-run, hurt the results of the first subsidiary and the entire group, he felt that "long-term profitability not only of the groups and of the second subsidiary, but also of the first subsidiary depended on the second country remaining in the trade liberalization agreement."[10]

Also in the mid-1970s, a subsidiary in a large country, which had been manufacturing Xerox's smaller machines, found that the demand for this product was declining. On the initiative of the area staff the country's manufacturing operations were converted from the assembly of new machines to the refurbishing of old ones. A number of Xerox managers, both locally and at headquarters, expressed concern that this might signal to the local government that the company was not serious about expanding its local manufacturing. There was some apprehension that the issuance of import licenses could be affected because of the country's concern with its balance of trade deficit. The conversion from manufacturing to refurbishing went through and was immediately followed by a slowdown in the issuance of licenses. Government officials pointed a finger at the cessation of manufacturing. When Xerox submitted plans to invest $20 million in local manufacturing of the "3107 copier," a more sophisticated machine than earlier copiers, import licenses for other products were restored. Local authorities specifically accepted the new investment proposal as a substitute for the discontinued manufacturing.

[10]Meyerson, *op. cit.*

Furthermore, in late 1977 a subsidiary in another large country found its pricing policies challenged by charges that a small locally owned competitor had made to the Ministry of Commerce. In response to pressure from the local competitor, the government doubled its tariffs on toner, the powder used in xerographic printing, which Xerox was importing, and closed the country's border to developers, which were also being imported. Thus the aggressive pricing policy in the country set by the Area Marketing Staff had drawn government reaction that had repercussions on the operations of other subsidiaries exporting to this subsidiary. Xerox's integrated network was being affected. Some country subsidiary managers had warned area management regarding the potential political dangers of pursuing an aggressive pricing policy, but the issue had not surfaced as a significant government-relations risk at headquarters and had not affected the formulation of marketing strategies. It took more than a year of negotiations for the damage to be repaired; henceforth Xerox had agreed to adhere to specific pricing instructions issued by the Ministry of Commerce. The cost of being reactive was high: an important marketing decision, namely pricing, was now subject to constant negotiations with the government!

These instances, among others, drove home to corporate top management the incompatibility between pursuing an integrated strategy requiring regionally centralized decision making and coordination and a reactive approach toward management of government issues. Although the operating logic of the Area Functional Staff overseeing an integrated system was dominated by economic considerations, management recognized the need to reconcile it with a more anticipatory and organized approach to management of government issues.

The issues Xerox faced were varied, and although the impact of each was decidedly modest continuation of a reactive approach would only result in further crises down the road; and the effect of even a small issue could look decidedly big because of its disruptive escalating impact on other units of an interdependent multinational network. Not wishing to effect a fundamental change in the international strategy toward a country-oriented approach, it was decided to initiate a formal government-issues reporting and information system with the primary purpose of surfacing issues early enough so that a timely response could be affected.

1977–1981: In Transition

The prime mover of a more formalized and anticipatory approach in managing government issues at corporate headquarters was Robert M. Pippitt, Senior Vice-President for Corporate Affairs. Pippitt had impressive credentials as senior line manager in the company's international operations, having formerly served as Managing Director and Chief Executive for Rank Xerox (1970–1974) and later as Group Vice-President with responsibility for Xerox Latin America Group and Xerox of Canada. In 1977 he was responsible for public relations, employee communications, and civic and government affairs throughout Xerox's operations. Together with the Chairman, the President, and three Executive Vice-Presidents, he was one of six members of the Corporate Policy Committee, which reviewed all major operating and investment decisions made by Xerox worldwide. Later in 1977, in a memorandum distributed to Xerox executives, he proposed the establishment of a Corporate Affairs International Advisory Board (CAIAB) within each of the operating groups—namely, Rank Xerox, Xerox Latin America, Fuji Xerox, and Xerox Canada—as well as a similar board on a corporate-wide basis. In addition, an international monitoring system involving country managers was to be instituted.

In his memorandum Pippitt observed that "significant issues in the government relations area" were not being handled formally but rather "by crisis management leading to the establishment of a task force or an ad hoc committee to handle critical matters." He went on to say:

> Clearly, many functional organizations in the operating groups are directly concerned and involved in corporate affairs matters which make communications very complex and unresponsive to the forecasting and analytical needs of government relations.
>
> Many of the issues which the Corporate Affairs International Advisory Board would have on its agenda are today solved by crisis management. . . .[11]

In 1978 the Latin American Group, where Xerox's problems had been the most acute, became, appropriately enough, the first operating group in which a formalized government-issues monitoring system and CAIAB were instituted. Pippitt formally suggested the idea before a quarterly meeting of country managing directors and regional staff directors, along with Dan Sharp, the group's Director of Inter-American Affairs, who was charged with facilitating the introduction.

The Issue Monitoring System—or IMS, as it was later called—required each country managing director to prepare a quarterly report detailing the ten most important issues for Xerox in the subsidiary's external environment, with their implications for Xerox operations, and a brief assessment of alternate action plans that should be considered. The report is sent to the line superior (an operations vice-president) and to the region's Director of Inter-American Affairs. In this way the system ensures that serious issues could be surfaced early and brought to the attention of higher levels of management.

Realizing from the outset that if the IMS were to be taken seriously, merely establishing an additional reporting requirement would not suffice. At Sharp's urging top management sanctioned the integration of IMS with the company's well established management-by-objectives system. Based on the quar-

[11]Meyerson, *op. cit.*

terly reports, the country managing director negotiated, with the operations vice-president, a list of proposed objectives with respect to government relations management. The annual performance review explicitly takes into account the extent to which the managing director has achieved those objectives. Thus IMS was integrated into the measurement and reward systems.

Further, to emphasize line management responsibility for government issues and to facilitate knowledge transfer within the region each country managing director presented an IMS report before quarterly meetings of country directors and regional staff managers. A summary of this report from these meetings was then presented at the corporatewide CAIAB, also established in 1978.

Xerox's formalized approach toward managing government issues clearly centered around the country manager, who was seen as having the prime responsibility for government relations. As Sharp put it:

> Our best sources are the local managers. They are better educated and informed about their environments than anyone here at staff headquarters. Often, they went to school with those who run the government and other important institutions in their countries.[12]

To buttress their added responsibility government-relations specialists were designated in major subsidiaries. Brazil had a staff of three; Mexico, two; Canada, the United Kingdom, France, Germany, Italy, and Sweden, one each; some specialists were part-time. These staffs are responsible to the country manager.

At first glance the great emphasis on formally establishing the responsibilities of line management, especially country

[12]Quoted in "The Multinationals Get Smarter About Political Risks," Fortune, March 24, 1980.

managers, may seem misplaced in the light of the crisis inci-
dents experienced by Xerox in the diffuse phase. The decision
to downgrade a country manufacturing facility to refurbishing
old machines and the aggressive pricing policies that triggered
the wrath of two governments were made primarily by the regional functional staffs based in Greenwich, Connecticut—not
by country managers. In fact, in both cases country managers
had foreseen and warned of potentially negative reactions by
their governments. The well placed warnings had been ignored.

Now, via the IMS, the country manager's perspective acquired a formal prominence it had never had. The regional
functional staffs could no longer ignore the recommendations
made. Neither could they simply overrule them. They were
now forced to engage in negotiations with country managers
and operations vice-presidents whenever they disagreed with
their assessments. Because the responsibility of country managers was formally consecrated into the measurement and reward
systems, the country managers acquired the implicit authority
to protest functional decisions and escalate the issues to higher
levels of management.

In addition, they were, for the first time, provided with a
channel for initiating functional strategies such as the local
manufacture of some components. One country manager's report contained the following recommendations:

Manufacture toner locally for export

Think of assembling machines

Company balance of payments is negative, both short- and long-
range, under present plans; no real improvement in next few
years

If required balance of payments positive for Xerox corporate
presence, we must:

(a) Substantially increase exports in the next 10 years

(b) Correspondingly decrease imports

(c) Increase equity investment.

Food for thought for regional functional staffs and grist for the planning process! Thus the new administrative mechanisms enhanced the authority of the country manager and made certain that government issues were incorporated into the area and corporate decision-making and planning process. By promoting and ensuring the country managers' views in this way it also ensured that implementation of a response would be harmonious.

Rewarding country managers on their government relations performances and subjecting them to peer review was a way of making sure that they identified themselves with the company's interests. The country managers' power, in the long-run, depended on their credibility. The record of subsidiary managers' assessments of government issues was a key to their credibility. Managers were thus likely to remain sensitive to the balance between economic and government imperatives.

The objectives set for country managers as part of the MBO system were, of necessity, process-oriented. For instance, the government-relations targets of one country manager contained the following:

Assure the import of 3100 machines

Negotiate manufacturing expansion projects with National Industrial Development Ministry

To help balance of payments, offer to book important equipment as capital investment rather than as purchase from overseas

Establish and maintain effective relations with the new government and with its key people as well as career officials.

It was against these process-oriented objectives that performance was evaluated.

The IMS, with its emphasis on surfacing serious issues early, bringing them to the attention of appropriate levels of management, and providing an early warning system, serves two major purposes: first, it permits the company to understand likely

changes required in company operations and procedures early
enough to result in effective adaptation; second, in rare cases it
could allow the company to influence results when appropriate
and feasible while the issue is in the early stages of its life
cycle.

In 1980, after having overseen the establishment of the IMS
in Latin America, Dan Sharp was promoted to the post of Director of International Relations at corporate headquarters. From
this position he supervised the worldwide introduction of the
systems in Rank Xerox and other operating groups. He describes his role then:

> I saw myself as a catalyst in facilitating the system changes in
> Latin America. . . . My basic role now is to manage the IMS pro-
> cess and insure effective input from the field. I act as a conduit
> making sure that corporate management is informed of results of
> field work and the CAIAB meetings. In some ways, my most im-
> portant task, as I see it, is to act as a strategy provocateur. I dis-
> cuss issues, function-by-function and with line management,
> making sure all major functions understand the issues.

> I feel that Corporate Affairs has a role in identifying emergent is-
> sues from the environment which could have direct impact on
> Xerox and therefore could become business problems. Once an
> issue has been identified and recognized by senior management
> and functional staffs as a business problem, the responsibility
> for managing our response to that issue lies with the appropri-
> ate operating group or staff function. The corporate affairs role
> reverts to that of monitoring new developments and new as-
> pects.[13]

In keeping with this philosophy, the corporate and regional
government affairs staffs were small. Rank Xerox had a staff of
two persons; Latin America and Canada, one each.

By mid-1981 the Issue Monitoring System had been fully in-

[13]Personal communication.

tegrated into Xerox's information and planning system. Government issues raised by IMS provide valuable input into the corporate strategic planning process and operating plans explicitly address priority IMS issues.

The worldwide and operating group CAIAB provided a useful forum that met twice a year for discussion of government issues and transfer of information and experience between operating groups and countries. The goal of these meetings, in Pippitt's words, was "to exchange information about the political trends that might develop in some regions earlier than others, so that managers in Latin America, for example, would learn about political ideas originating in Western Europe that might spread elsewhere." The CAIAB meetings were also designed "to help bring information about trends in the external environment directly into corporate planning." Pippitt would present a summary of the CAIAB proceedings before meetings of the Corporate Policy Committee.

Thus in a span of just four years Xerox had developed an institutionalized anticipatory approach toward the management of government relations. As a result of top management's desire to avoid the costs of a reactive approach and its consequent commitment to the systematic management of government issues new administrative systems had been established and incorporated into the management-by-objectives evaluation system. The awareness and necessity of dealing with government issues had been instilled in line and functional managers and the IMS had input into the corporate planning system.

There was nothing piecemeal or haphazard about the way this "bottom-up" system had been implemented. It reflected the managerial initiative and values of Pippitt, who was a prime mover behind the system. Pippitt brought to bear his wide experience in line management of overseas operations to his job in Corporate Affairs. As a member of top corporate management he was able to allocate corporate resources to ensure its successful insertion into the organizational body politic.

To be sure, Xerox had not yet developed policies on the major issues that it faced. In part, this was due to the variety of issues with which it was confronted. What the formalized system did do was provide a process by which issues were raised to the appropriate level in the organization and ensure that timely responses could be made. It relied primarily on the formal operating group structure involving functional staff and line managers to deal with issues. When issues cut across operating groups, ad hoc teams would be set up to design corporate responses. As an internal report noted, however, Xerox had not yet grappled with such questions as how to evaluate the global impact on Xerox of each proposed response to government pressures for local manufacture and local value-added. Thus the potential existed that in spite of significant attention to government issues the sum of different corporate responses to specific issues might result in disjointed and incremental adjustments in its integrated strategy, with attendant costs.

In some ways it could be argued that Xerox now resembled the Structured Mode more than the Assertive. In an initial evaluation of how the system was working an internal assessment report expressed satisfaction with the impact of the system on management of government issues in Latin America, where it had been introduced. Sharp's personal evaluation was equally positive:

> Though we still have some serious problems, they haven't become crises lately because the issues affecting our business are dealt with much earlier.[14]

1981: Diversification into Salience

In 1981, even as Xerox was growing confident of its ability to manage government issues, it was beginning to experience an

---

[14]"The Multinationals Get Smarter . . . ," op. cit.

entirely different set of government issues that seemed to call for major strategic and structural adaptation. As the various strategic business units of its fledgling Office Products Division (OPD) established overseas operations in order to gain a foothold in the European automated office equipment market, they found the going rough. Nothing in their U.S. experience had prepared them for dealing with government-owned PTTs, which were positioned as dominant actors in the industry Europeans called "telematics," and the extensive national government regulations on transborder information and data flows.

Throughout the 1970s Xerox's goal had been to establish itself as an office systems company, not just a specialist in copiers. Toward that goal Xerox had embarked on an ambitious acquisitions program that involved small, high-technology, U.S. firms specializing in microelectronics, computer memories, and floppy-disk drives. Together with its own research center in Palo Alto, these companies, under the rubric of the Office Products Division, had developed automated electronic work stations, software programs, sophisticated information processors, electronic typewriters with memory features, and a family of telecopiers with greatly increased transmission speed. In 1980 Xerox announced its capstone product: Ethernet, a coaxial cable network designed to link together all elements of an automated office. Xerox was now operating in a business that spanned the boundary between data processing and telecommunications—a highly salient sector in Europe.

Though office products sales accounted for only 10% of Xerox's $8 billion in sales in 1981, Massaro, President of OPD, stated that Xerox's future depends on success in the automated office.

> The corporation must be successful in this marketplace. We don't have a choice. We're not Exxon. We can't go out and drill another oil well.[15]

[15]Quoted in "The New Lean, Mean Xerox," Business Week, October 21, 1981.

Corporate executives expected very high growth in the new product lines and estimated that company sales would increase threefold in the next five years.

However, the initial overseas foray of Xerox's U.S. subsidiaries in this field had driven home some stunning lessons. The telecopier 485 was blocked in France, Germany, and Spain, and all of Ethernet and its associated products could be affected similarly. Already Holland was insisting on buying Ethernet cable and then leasing it back to Xerox. Canada's electrical installation codes hindered the introduction of Ethernet and the autodial feature of telecopier 485 had been blocked. Indeed, as an IMS document put it, "the risk to Xerox is being blocked from participating in 'office of the future' market in most countries overseas."

What happened, of course, was that Xerox was unprepared by the dominance of state-owned PTTs which set technical standards (e.g., for interface equipment), determine tariff schedules (punitive on international traffic), and could bar foreign suppliers through purchasing policy. This sense of surprise was, in part, due to the fact that office-product subsidiaries in the United States were marketing their products directly in Europe and not through the Rank Xerox organization.

Now it was clear that much of Xerox's future would be based on products that had to be approved, bought by, and installed with PTTs (one estimate: 50%). In addition, countries, especially France, had earmarked an $8 to 10 billion fund for developing a national industry in office products and foreign firms could possibly be excluded.

Xerox had been slow to react. As of mid-1981 it was unclear what international strategy Xerox would pursue in office products and how it could organize its overseas operations. Answers to those two questions would have to revolve around how Xerox proposed to manage its dealings with governments and PTTs. Two broad, extreme courses of action were available. First, Xerox could develop and offer substantive trade-offs (like

IBM) attractive enough to induce PTTs to accept Xerox as a local market participant. Xerox was just beginning to develop specific plans to identify its bargaining position. Clearly, it was still far from specifying what it could offer.

On the other hand, Xerox could opt for a country-oriented strategy of national accommodation, like ITT. What would this imply for management of government relations? For IMS?

Perhaps as a portent of what is to follow, in February 1982 Xerox announced an agreement with Siemens A.G., the major West German electronics and telecommunications giant, to work together to develop and market integrated office systems. Siemens would integrate the Xerox local area network Ethernet and compatible Xerox 8000 systems products into its PABX-oriented switching product line. Siemens would market the systems in West Germany, Austria, and Switzerland—countries in which it had well established telecommunications operations.

If this is reflective of future strategy, it may indicate that top management has decided on a joint venture with well established European telecommunications firms which would then help to handle dealings with PTTs. In this way Xerox will have finessed the need to develop a government-relations strategy and structure suited to the needs of a highly salient industry.

National government regulation of cross-border information and data flows was a recently emergent issue that had begun to affect Xerox in its existing operations. Government concern with information rights had led to the adoption of diverse information control regimes. Government pressures had already forced Rank Xerox to decentralize some data processing in Europe which had earlier been centralized to reduce costs and increase efficiency. Eventually this could entail the abandonment of Xerox's Internal Data Processing network and the reestablishment of separate country facilities.

The trend in national regulations was even more ominous. After 1984 all corporate data about Germany was to be processed locally. Canada, too, had imposed a similar requirement. France was planning to base its tax on cross-border flows, not on quantity but on value of data! This would mean giving customs officials access to data.

These developments were creating uncertainty for some of Xerox's customers. Xerox was highly concerned about the implications for its freedom to operate the "office of the future" under new laws.

Xerox's Issue Monitoring System had identified Trans-Border Data Flows (TBDFs) as a high-priority issue and regulatory developments in this sphere were being regularly assessed as they affected Xerox as user and manufacturer. A special corporatewide meeting of executives had been held in April 1981 to examine this one issue. Operating companies were required to submit special reports on TBDF developments.

Corporate top management was constantly kept abreast of new developments by Corporate Affairs Staff, for new developments could substantially affect top management's plans for new R&D projects and marketing strategy for the "office of the future" and internal data processing networks.

Like IBM, Xerox believed that there was an opportunity for a coordinated proactive involvement to influence government regulatory thinking, especially through support of efforts by international organizations, such as OECD, to harmonize the present differences in national laws. A senior manager, with a mastery of the technical issues involved, was eventually appointed as an "issue control officer" for TBDF. He was to serve as the focal point of efforts within the company to keep abreast of developments around the world, to help develop policy and to represent the company in numerous private sector and government committees dealing with the issue.

Thus, as Xerox entered the 1980s, it was confronted with a substantially different set of government issues arising from its entry into the high-technology salient businesses. The extent to which it would be successful in attaining its proclaimed goal of becoming a leading international office systems company by the end of this decade would, in large measure, depend on its ability to manage these government issues. It was becoming clear that, by itself, a highly formalized Issue Monitoring System was not a panacea and could not substitute for the development of substantive responses to these emergent issues. IMS could surface issues early and relied on the regular structure to deal with them as they came up. As long as the area management and functional staffs had familiarity with issues, they could fashion case-specific responses without the guidance of policies on government issues. At least a codified set of past practices and experience served as guides. However, as Xerox's product mix shifts toward the more salient businesses, experience does not provide much help.

It would also be well to remember that Xerox was moving into industry sectors that housed IBM and ITT. Both practice an assertive approach to government-relations management, albeit with significant differences, and each had developed its own system over decades of experience. Could Xerox rise to the challenge?

4

The Structured Mode

STRUCTURED MODE DEFINED

In the Structured Mode government power dominates both industry and company affairs. Host governments not only dictate terms to companies but also control large sections of the industry itself. In such a situation all issues are open to negotiation and the negotiation process is continuous.

With the continual need to adjust and readjust company policy to government demands, the government-relations strategies of Structured companies tend to be almost indistinguishable from overall operational strategies of the firm: management of company relations with governments that control the fundamental aspects of their existence easily translates into the management of the business itself. Moreover, as strategy is the force behind structure, the dominance of government power is reflected in the development of highly structured systems and processes for the management of government issues—both within the formal organizational structure of the firm and between the company and the bureaucracy.

The dominance of government power over the activities of

131

Structured companies is reflected in two fundamental strategy/ structure contrasts with the Assertive Mode: (1) the necessity for piecemeal and ongoing negotiations with host-country officials and (2) the consequent "functionalization" of government-relations processes and structures.

Unlike the Assertive companies of Chapter 2, companies in the Structured Mode are unable to impose their will on host governments through centrally developed company policies or to seek a "negotiated environment" in which long-term trade-offs guarantee a certain continuity to company operations. Rather they must be prepared to bargain for any and all terms of operation. Company bargaining power in this Mode is defined around highly issue- and situation-specific events and is often realized only in a piecemeal and ad hoc manner.

Government-relations activities permeate the company organization, both line and staff. At the same time this need for continuous, negotiations across all issues has given rise to the development of a specific "Government Negotiations" function within the formal structure of the firm. Professional negotiations specialists represent company interests worldwide at the entry level and at the renegotiation stages of operations, drawing on other highly specialized government tax and legal specialists, and routinely assembling project teams around specific government issues.

Like many companies in the Assertive Mode, the formal organizational structure of these companies is also characterized by highly developed, corporate-wide systems and reporting procedures for the transfer of information from one area of the organization to the next. There is also a clear delineation of government-relations responsibilities at all levels of management. However, as with the degree of government power that separates them from the Assertive Mode, the distinction here is also one of magnitude: the organization of Structured companies around the "government imperative" is by far the most visible feature of the company policy and structure.

In light of the foregoing, the basic industry and structural characteristics of companies in this mode would be similar to those of the Assertive Mode—again with a significant qualitative difference in extent—in terms of the high degree of salience, the prevalence of integrated operational strategies, and the multinationality of their international networks. In our sample of 13 MNCs it was therefore not surprising that the only companies to fall into this mode were the international oil companies: Exxon, Socal, Mobil, Gulf, Arco, and Conoco. The following description of their operations characteristics will serve to highlight this point.

CHARACTERISTICS OF COMPANIES: CHALLENGES IN GOVERNMENT-RELATIONS MANAGEMENT

Influence of Salience

In terms of size, gross revenues, and impact on the world economy, the international oil industry is by far the most salient in the world. For more than a decade, since 1973, the global transactions involved in the oil trade have thrown the entire world economy off balance, with the high surpluses of the producing countries consistently reflected in the large deficits of nonproducing countries.

For the producing countries the revenues from the oil industry are significant, usually dwarfing government budgetary revenues from all other sources. Iran's oil income accounted for some 55% of its total budget revenues; in Kuwait, as much as 86%. Similarly, Pertamina, the Indonesian state-owned oil company, earned half that country's foreign exchange in the mid-1970s. This centrality of the oil industry to national economies is the cause and effect of the high government involvement in the industry.

The oil industry is one in which the power of host governments was clearly ascendant in the 1970s. Beginning in 1971, the producing country governments seized—and the oil companies lost—the power to determine prices of crude oil and the freedom to orchestrate their production levels. Prior to that time the major oil companies determined prices in response to market developments without deference to the wishes of producer governments. This resulted in a fall in prices in real terms for Middle East oil almost every year since 1947. The 1971 Tehran-Tripoli negotiations confirmed, for the first time, that host governments had the power to push through increases in posted prices against company wishes; and in October 1973, in the immediate aftermath of the Arab oil embargo, the Organization of Petroleum Exporting Countries (OPEC) took over the price-setting function completely—oil companies were no longer involved in pricing decisions.

At the same time participation became the major objective of the producing countries. This meant that companies were forced to relinquish the traditional concession agreements (which, among other things, permitted concession holders to determine production levels in the absence of specific provisions to the contrary) in favor of host-government participation in or outright nationalization of their upstream activities. Host governments came to acquire a decisive say in their production: their control of supply of their national oil resources is now complete.

The industry scene had undergone a sea change. A genuine revolution had taken place. Companies are increasingly required to accept the right of host governments to make—or at least to be seen making—strategic decisions at the upstream level.

On the operational level, however, producing governments have had to reach agreements with the multinational oil companies that still dominate key processes within the industry. For example, Saudi Arabia took a long time to formalize a 100% takeover of Aramco, though agreements were negotiated with the four parent companies in the early 1980s. While trying to maintain a sufficiently nationalistic approach on the surface the Saudis sought to engage these oil companies as partners in the development of the oil industry and other ambitious industrialization schemes. Even in Venezuela, where oil has been a burning political issue since the 1920s and which undertook a comprehensive nationalization program in 1975, the majors have been granted service contracts and receive privileged access to oil. Thus Exxon's Venezuelan subsidiary now operates as a government concern, LAGOVEN. Exxon provides technical assistance to LAGOVEN in return for fees based on rates of production of crude and natural gas liquids and refinery output. In addition, as part of the agreement, Exxon "loans" its exsubsidiary some 150 employees while local nationals are being trained. Thus even nationalization has not meant replacement of international oil companies with government-owned counterparts; rather countries have preferred to negotiate various arrangements in which a majority of marketing and technological questions are left to the oil companies. This is a result of a strategic choice to concentrate national resources on production (where the returns to the country are highest) and a recognition of company expertise in other areas.

A distinctive feature of the oil industry is the extent to which producer governments are organized—both internationally and within each country—to deal with the international oil companies. OPEC, founded in 1960, has contributed significantly to member governments' awareness and knowledge of industry affairs. It has institutionalized cooperation between host governments by providing a forum where countries can draw on one another's experience and a clearinghouse for ideas and information. This has clear implications for the management of government relations for oil companies. Because oil is a standardized commodity, such an information exchange enhances the capacity of producer governments to monitor terms of exploration and production agreements elsewhere and compare them to their own situations. Historically, once a company granted favorable terms to one country, it triggered demands for renegotiations from other countries which affected it as well as other companies in the industry. As an early example, in 1949 Saudi Arabia was quick to demand a 50-50 profit split, a concept that had been introduced in Venezuela in 1948 (desiring solidarity with major Middle East producers, the Venezuelans had translated their documents into Arabic and sent a diplomatic mission to the region to explain the principle) and the oil companies acceded. As a more momentous event, Occidental's cave-in to Libya's price demands in 1970 was the first ripple of the price avalanche that blasted through the industry. It was expressly to avoid "leapfrogging" or "ratcheting" between the Libyans and the Gulf states that the oil companies banded together in 1971 and decided to centralize their negotiations with host governments. Their intentions were expressed in a joint letter to OPEC:

> We have concluded that we cannot further negotiate the development of claims by member countries of OPEC on any other basis than one which reaches a settlement simultaneously with all producing governments concerned. It is therefore our proposal that an all-embracing negotiation should be commenced between representatives of ourselves . . . on the one hand, and OPEC as representing all its Member Countries on the other hand, under which an overall and durable settlement could be achieved.[1]

OPEC refused to engage in a single global negotiation and the worst fears of the companies came to pass. A few countries even inserted "most favored nation" clauses in their agreements providing for the automatic application of the terms of any sub-

---

[1]Text of a letter included in Frank Church's report, "Multinational Oil Corporation and U.S. Foreign Policy," together with individual views, to the Committee on Foreign Relations, U.S. Senate, by the Subcommittee on Multinational Corporations (Washington: U.S. Government Printing Office, 1975).

sequent agreement the company might reach with other countries if those terms were more favorable to the government.

Thus government issues confronting oil companies have great precedent-setting potential and can escalate to affect company and industry interests across the world. As such, the company–government-relations processes must provide for centralized assessment of the implications of a substantive response by senior executives who can bring to bear a corporate-wide perspective.

Even though OPEC did serve briefly as a collective bargaining force between 1971 and 1974, individual host governments as a rule negotiate their own agreements with individual companies. In addition to having well developed petroleum laws, mature producing countries have established specialized oil bureaucracies consisting of national oil companies (NOCs) and a cabinet-level Ministry of Petroleum. The development of national oil companies with a cadre of trained engineers and a core of managers who are charged with overseeing the domestic oil industry and the local operations of international oil companies connotes a coming-of-age for the producing countries. Most NOCs exhibit specialized structures through which all dealings with foreign firms are conducted. The Department of International Affairs in the National Iranian Oil Company and Pertamina in Indonesia are two examples. In Saudi Arabia responsibility for dealing with private companies involves Petromin, the state oil company, and the Oil Ministry. The Oil Ministers, in the main, represent their countries at OPEC forums and it is they who meet regularly to set prices or, in rare cases, to decide on production ceilings and allocations (as happened in 1981 and throughout 1986).

The necessity of dealing with a group of national oil company managers and staff (a "company-relations" function, as it were) who are primarily responsible for negotiating with, and supervising, operations of the international oil companies finds reflection in the development of matching government-relations structures on the part of the companies. Thus all oil companies tend to have government negotiations specialists comprised of full-time negotiators and other staff who are drawn together in a team each time negotiations are undertaken.

Influence of Company Strategy

Since the very early days of the industry the oil business has been dominated by vertically integrated firms. The four operational stages—production of crude, processing, transportation, and marketing—are all highly vulnerable to market supply-and-demand conditions. In surplus years producers need guaranteed markets and in shortage years refiners need guaranteed sources and outlets. Global expansion strategies over the last century have been characterized by these two fundamental considerations.

Because crude oil is basically undifferentiated, the most logical way to organize international operations is on a worldwide functional basis, with specialized divisions for each of the four major production stages. Four of the six firms in our samples —Mobil, Gulf, Atlantic Richfield (Arco), and Conoco[2]—are functionally organized. Typically, the functional divisions are grouped as follows: Exploration and Production (E&P), Marketing and Refining (M&R), Trading and Transportation (T&T), and Chemicals. Socal,[3] because of its nearly half-century-old joint venture with Texaco, another major, is organized on somewhat different lines. Exploration and production activities are carried out by three groups, each overseeing specific areas or countries around the world. Most worldwide marketing and refining is undertaken by Caltex, another 50-50 joint venture with Texaco.

[2]Conoco was acquired by DuPont in September 1981.
[3]Standard Oil of California, or Socal, formally changed its name to Chevron Corporation on July 1, 1984. This followed the acquisition of Gulf by Socal in March 1984. Socal is the term generally used throughout this chapter.

Exxon is organized quite differently. The biggest oil company in the world, with probably the largest network of international operations, is organized geographically: Exxon Middle East, Esso Inter-America, Esso Eastern, Esso Europe, Esso U.S.A., and Exxon International. Each geographic division has a full complement of functional staffs.

A significant aspect of the international quest for sources and markets was the development of complex interlocking patterns of investments and agreements between the oil companies. This pattern evolved historically as a result of risk-reducing, matching moves made by the different majors and was formalized in agreements that doled out territorial rights. Country-oriented consortia or joint ventures, such as the Iranian Oil Consortium, Aramco in Saudi Arabia, and BP-Gulf arrangements in Kuwait, have given way to the modern version—the formation of partnerships to bid for the rights to specific blocks (the days of exclusive country concessions having been long gone), which are essentially project-oriented joint ventures. Usually, in such cases, a major partner is elected to be the managing operator, with production being shared according to individual company interest in the venture.

The implications of such arrangements for company management of government relations are fairly obvious. These consortia/joint-venture arrangements provide a legitimate forum for the involved firms to coordinate their actions and policies toward host governments. In conjunction with the formal attempts made between 1971 and 1973 by international oil companies to act in concert and to centralize their dealings with OPEC countries—efforts that were blessed with antitrust exemptions by U.S. authorities and which resulted in the establishment of a policy-coordinating body called the London Policy Group, made up of senior executives of U.S. and European oil companies—such intercompany arrangements forced companies toward common positions and action plans. This helps to explain why different oil companies tend to have similar strategies and structures for dealing with governments. Indeed, viewed in this light, it is not at all surprising that there is great homogeneity in behavior across companies.

The 1970s saw the companies being forced to enter into service contracts, production-sharing agreements, or joint ventures whereby the international oil companies offer some combination of technology, markets, and skilled personnel in return for a share of the production or some combination of fees or preferentially priced crude. It is rare for companies to have any equity stake in producing facilities in the mature, established producing countries. (Equity production, though, still exists in the newly emerging oil countries such as Angola, Sudan, and Somalia.)

As companies lost control over the supply of crude oil, they began reexamining their roles as integrated companies. Some companies divested themselves of their unprofitable downstream operations. Gulf has retrenched from marketing and refining operations in Latin America, Korea, and Germany. Exxon pulled out of India and the Philippines.

Company strategies in the future promise to be heavily conditioned by the policies of host governments. As governments have become the prime actors determining the overall strategies of major investments, oil companies have found themselves in a supporting role, supplying markets, management, capital, and finance or a "bundle of skills" as the circumstances demand. A significant part of their new role will involve serving the national governments or national oil companies. Opportunities for management control are likely to be substantially diluted by the extent of government participation or the terms of the management contract. The pattern of ownership in different stages of the industry will vary according to circumstance. The degree to which companies are able to integrate the various operations involved will depend on the desires of the different governments or national oil companies involved. In other words, integration will have to be negotiated with multiple partners rather than determined by control of company decisions alone.

Two broad strategic paths can be discerned. The first draws its inspiration from the phrase, "problems and opportunities are two sides of the same coin." OPEC countries may have sharply curtailed the role of the international oil company, but their plans for investing their new-found wealth in infrastructure, petrochemical complexes and general large-scale projects are alluring prospects for the majors that seek to take advantage of their technology and historical ties. This would, perhaps, increase their dependency on host countries, but it would also increase the dependency of the host on the company. If a company has built a $2-billion petrochemical complex in Saudi Arabia, it might be that the Saudis are now more dependent on the company than vice versa, for the country will have to rely on the company to provide an export market for the output of the complex. Such a strategy may also be based on the company's desire to have an assured access to long-term crude suppliers. This path would accentuate the feeling of living in a constantly negotiable environment, though the rewards of partnership may be substantial.

The second broad strategy calls for diverting capital into new geographic areas or businesses. Some companies have substantially enhanced the portion of their exploration budget spent in the politically predictable and stable countries of North America and Western Europe (even though the companies in these countries are chafing at such unilateral government acts as the new Canadian energy policy which discriminates against foreign companies and the United Kingdom's retrospective increase in the Petroleum Revenue Tax by 10% in 1981). A few have turned their energies to diversification within the United States (the "fortress U.S.A. syndrome") and have undertaken investments in other energy and mineral sectors such as coal, shale oil, copper, and aluminum. But, to the extent that they still have oil interests overseas, they too are likely to continue to exhibit a structured approach toward government-relations management.

Influence of Spread

The international network of oil companies generally tends to be vast, though there are substantial differences in the extent of spread between companies. Exxon boasts of having been a multinational some 50 years before that term came into popular use. With the most widespread network of all oil companies, Exxon has exploration and production activities in 41 countries, marketing and refining in close to a hundred. The complex logistical system operated by Exxon's computers involves maneuvering 500 ships from 115 loading ports to 270 destinations carrying 160 different crude oils to 65 countries. Socal, Mobil, and Gulf, too, have extensive exploration activities in some 40, 15, and 10 countries, respectively, and marketing operations in scores more. Recently, though, Gulf has been divesting itself from substantial foreign chunks of its downstream operations. Arco and Conoco are international primarily in the exploration and production stages (six countries each), with downstream operations being largely concentrated in the United States.

The generally broad spread of international operations of these companies illustrates the opportunities for benefiting from the development of organization mechanisms to capture substantial economies of learning and experience transfer. Given the necessity of constantly negotiating every aspect of their operations, companies with a broad spread are more likely to develop specialized structures or provide more depth in existing structures to ensure their ability to sense opportunities, marshal resources, assess risks, and determine how any response fits into overall corporate strategy in the course of developing situation-specific responses on government issues. At the extreme an oil company that is a newcomer to international operations with, say, just two countries in which it has exploration operations is more likely to be in the Diffuse Mode of managing government relations rather than the Structured. In other words, it will have more in common with Cummins than with Mobil or Gulf or Arco. The scale of its international operations will be insufficient to support specialized staff such as professional negotiators. Indeed, senior executives are likely to be involved in actual dealings with host governments even over routine issues. The companies in our sample, however, all seemed to have crossed the threshold necessary, in terms of spread and size of international operations, to have the required specialized personnel. Even Arco and Conoco, the two independents that are relatively less multinational than the four majors, had gone overseas in the 1950s and had experienced the full range of government demands during the 1970s. As such, there are no significant differences between the smaller and larger companies studied in their management of government relations. Where the companies sometimes differed—and rather dramatically at that—was in their choice of substantive response, which is affected by the overall strategy, resources, and risk profile of senior management, factors that can vary across companies.

GOVERNMENT-RELATIONS STRATEGY

With the ascendance of government power over the production stage, an effective government-relations strategy has become tantamount to survival in the international oil business. Companies must now be prepared to find political solutions to economic problems at every stage of company operations, from the negotiation of a new exploration agreement to the construction of a new refining facility.

In simple terms the fundamental change of the last decade

has been the radical split of the oil industry chain into halves: governments are now firmly in control of upstream activities (they set prices, determine production levels, set contract terms, etc.), whereas downstream activities are still firmly in company hands. As the halves of an integrated whole, however, neither can remain in the oil business without the active cooperation of the other: refineries and markets need guaranteed supplies of oil, just as oil wells and pipelines need guaranteed markets for their crude. Thus, whereas the oil politics of the early 1970s drew sharp adversarial lines between them, the simple economics of the industry has brought them together into a working—if tenuous—partnership.

Company-government relations in the 1980s can be characterized as a tenuous balance of power between government control of crude supplies on the one hand and company control of technology and markets on the other. In such a situation bargaining power is primarily determined by which end of the vertical chain is under consideration: for example, if the proposal is for a new exploration contract, the host government generally calls the shots, but when the offer is for joint-venture participation in a national refinery project the company usually has more leverage and more scope to formulate its own terms and conditions.

This division of power is by no means absolute: in a dynamic negotiating environment each side continually attempts to link its own specific power and expertise in one stage or area to favorable outcomes in other stages or areas—to extend its control, if you will. In an industry in which economics calls for vertical integration of operations this type of linkage bargaining has become a major feature of the negotiations process. For example, in a new explorations negotiation a company with special explorations know-how is in a good position to bargain for a better long-term supply agreement; or in a discussion to set up a joint-venture shipping company the government with the biggest share of company supplies could easily persuade management to lend a hand.

The distribution of power and control in the oil industry necessitates two separate strategies for the management of government relations: at the upstream level company strategy must clearly be of "national accommodation," whereas at the downstream level, where they still retain considerable control over operations, companies can generally afford to seek a negotiated environment similar to the long-term, company-government understandings in the Assertive Mode.

The most significant changes of the 1970s took place at the production end of the vertical chain, as governments continued to exercise their sovereign rights over the oil fields and wells in their territories. Once the wheels were set in motion, foreign oil companies essentially lost all guarantees to production rights and were forced to accept a continual hardening of contract terms, which, depending on the situation, ranged anywhere from higher taxes and decreased equity shares to the outright nationalization of their assets and the formation of national oil companies instead.

For those companies still operating rigs and wells in producing countries government-relations strategies must accommodate any and all government demands. In the last decade companies have gone from title bearers over large stretches of ocean and real estate to competitive bidders for small squares on a geographic grid. In new exploration negotiations the onus is entirely on the company to make its case and defend its bid against potential competitors. Thus, despite their technological expertise and willingness to finance high-risk ventures, "national accommodation" is still the most important government-relations strategy in oil explorations negotiations. This does not imply a passive acceptance of all claims to sovereignty: because of their continued access to markets and technologies, companies can still enjoy considerable bargaining strength vis-à-vis host governments.

For example, despite its captive status in the country, Arco's multicompany joint venture with the NIOC in Iran was able to hold off government demands for increased taxes for more than two and one-half years (from 1974 to 1977), by which time the price of crude had risen to a sufficient level to justify it in the company's eyes. Their position was, "If you want to nationalize us, go ahead, we will be no worse off," which effectively convinced the government that the loss of Arco's management and market access would be a poor trade-off for increased revenues.

Perhaps the most significant factor in the bargaining equation is the prevailing international supply-and-demand condition for oil and petroleum products. For example, in times of shortage producing governments are able to raise prices and harden terms significantly, whereas in the recent supply glut of 1986 the OPEC hardliners, like Libya and Nigeria, have seen their markets dwindle to dangerously low levels as companies switched to cheaper sources of supplies.

Oil companies also have to deal with the attempts of producing governments to use their control over crude to achieve forward linkages into downstream operations. When the market is with them, as it was in the second oil crisis (1978–1979), governments often achieve considerable success in this effort. Gulf dryly reported the exercise of host-government power in the industry with the following description of national oil policies in its 1979 Annual Report:

> With higher crude oil prices, producing nations can finance their foreign exchange requirements and development programs with less production today than a year ago, and are making unprecedented demands on prospective buyers as a condition of selling their crude. To obtain supplies, Gulf and other oil companies are being asked to make costly advance cash payments, undertake exploration and production activities, charter tankers at higher than commercial rates, transfer technology, and participate in processing and marketing ventures. Furthermore, some producers are imposing limitations on where and to whom crude can be sold.[4]

In seeking to harness the cooperation of oil companies in various downstream and other industrialization projects, govern-

[4]Gulf Oil Corporation, *Annual Report*, 1979.

ments do not rely on the "stick," but employ "carrots" as well. Substantial inducements are offered to companies in the form of incentive crude and generous financing terms.

Companies, for their part, appear to be willing to serve as skill banks and joint-venture partners for government projects. Their first objective, of course, is the opportunity to secure access to guaranteed crude supplies at favorable rates; however, with huge profits of their own, the opportunities for lucrative investments in producing-country industrialization projects are not lost on them.

With existing ties and a high tolerance for industrial cross-linkages, the oil companies are natural partners for the new development projects of the host countries. Thus ARAMCO is currently managing a $15-billion natural-gas project in Saudi Arabia that will provide a national base for investments in other heavy industries such as petrochemicals and iron ore processing. BP has deepened its ties to virtually all the producer countries in which it does business, with projects such as a 50-50 joint-venture tanker operation with the NIOC in Iran to a minority participation in a 100,000-ton/yr protein-farm-oil plant in Venezuela.[5]

Mobil has distinguished itself as the oil company most committed to producing-country development, with millions of dollars invested in some ten different industrialization projects throughout Saudi Arabia. The most significant of these is the development of the Red Sea port of Yanbu, where a new 800-mile pipeline terminates at a new petrochemical complex and export refinery.

New partnerships mean new complexities in company-government relations and the consequent rethinking of government-relations strategies.

To begin with, company participation in development projects entails the complex reconciliation of political ambitions

[5]Louis Turner, *Oil Companies in the International System* (Allen and Unwin, London, 1978).

cum national pride with business realism and the economic bottom line. This appears to be especially significant in the new petrochemical joint ventures, with oil companies already closing plants around the world to cut their losses from overcapacity.

In their diversification into new business fields, such as ventures in mining, the most serious question is the adaptability of oil company management and technology to the often significantly different problems of mining base metals. For example, oil companies take the biggest risk at the exploration phase: getting oil out of the ground is comparatively simple. However, the largest financial and operational problems of the mining industry begin only after the deposits are located. Moreover, the real rate of return is claimed by oil men to be only a third to one-half of the return on investment in oil.

These new complexities can extend very easily into the political sphere as companies try to adjust their government-relations strategies in oil to their new strategies in diversified joint ventures. For example, after Arco decided to make a strategic commitment to diversification in coal it targeted the government of Indonesia as its prime partner. Arco approached the negotiations process by following its tried and true oil politics without considering the possible differences that could arise with coal. First of all, it negotiated directly with the state coal company, Batubara, rather than the relevant government ministries, just as it handled most of its negotiations in oil with Pertamina, the state oil company. Batubara, however, had no real authority to negotiate but acted rather as a conduit for the Ministry of Mines and other government departments whose consent was necessary for any deal. After one and one-half years of negotiations the Arco team finally reached an agreement to enter into a joint-venture, production-sharing project with Batubara, only to have the plan vetoed by senior government officials. Only after senior executives of the corporation made personal approaches to senior ministers did the government appoint a Senior Coordinator to oversee future negotiations. It took another year and a half of negotiations before a deal was finally signed.

Another complexity of the new company-government partnerships of the 1980s stems from the high visibility of the oil companies themselves. Although they often make logical partners, they do not necessarily make popular ones. For example, after the state coal company of Colombia awarded Exxon a contract in 1980 a major public furor broke out over the operating terms to which they agreed. Parliamentary investigations were launched and all negotiations for further concessions halted. As a result, Arco—another interested company that, after three years of negotiations, had been close to an agreement on a coal concession in an adjoining area—found itself thwarted. In 1981 Arco management felt that it would require at least two years before they could renew their efforts.

The new partnerships and the sense of mutual dependency between host and firm mean that both will be equally—not oppositely—affected by the external forces of supply and demand. In the 1980s these relations look to be increasingly precarious, as the industrialized nations reduce their dependence on oil as a basic energy source. Thus overall oil company strategies will become increasingly difficult to distinguish from specific government-relations strategies as companies and governments tie their fortunes together in the face of the new uncertainties.

GOVERNMENT-RELATIONS PROCESS

The basic mechanisms and procedures for the resolution of government issues showed a remarkable similarity across all six companies in our sample: all were characterized by the centralization of decision-making power in the hands of senior corporate management, and clear delineation of responsibilities and reporting procedures marked the management of government relations throughout the formal organization structure. The most distinctive feature of the government-relations processes in the six companies was the existence of specialized staff functions designed to handle government issues. The most significant was the specialized "Government Negotiations Staff," usually attached to the Exploration and Production Division, which had general responsibility for company–government negotiations throughout the world.

Though striking in its extent, this similarity of process and structure across companies can be readily explained when one considers the nature and importance of the issues with which they deal and the extent of the historical ties between them. For an international oil company nearly all government-related issues are important in terms of their overall financial and strategic impact on the firm. Similarly, the combination of vertically integrated networks and widespread government power in the industry has the effect of magnifying even the most routine local problems: any disruption upstream calls for compensating adjustments downstream, and the way in which a company responds in one local situation can easily "leapfrog" through OPEC channels to other companies and other countries. Fifty years of history of various joint ventures and consortia arrangements between the major companies have also left their mark in the development of parallel organization structures and processes.

Despite the fundamental interrelatedness of issues that confront them and the similarity of process and structure, one can observe a diversity of substantive responses and outcomes across companies. This, as we shall see, is primarily a function of the differences in strategic postures, resources, and risk profiles between companies and where they would like to concentrate and deploy their resources. For all firms, however, government relations remain as the central feature of life, requiring them to be constantly prepared to respond quickly and flexibly from one situation to the next.

Managing Broad Issues

It is significant to note that most government-related issues that confront the oil companies have a broad reach, both geographically and functionally. In a vertically integrated production network local disruptions tend to require compensating adjustments farther down the line; and, given OPEC's widespread and sophisticated information network, any company response in one area can have a precedent-setting impact on the next.

Another dimension of the concept of "reach" that is not found in the other two government-relations modes is the tendency for issues in one company to have an impact on the actions of another. This, again, is the cause of close ties between the international oil companies and the dominance of government and OPEC power in the industry.

As in Assertive companies, "narrow" or local government-related issues are generally handled by the local management itself. These include such country-specific issues as employment levels, environmental protection laws, and compliance with local industrial rules. Typically, country managers of downstream operations are also responsible for dealing with host government officials to ensure the requisite price increases that are so vital to the profitability of marketing and refining activities of oil companies.

However, because oil companies frequently enter into joint ventures with local interests in downstream operations, they do not always rely on the local venture management to represent their interests. For example, Gulf established a separate office with a seven-man staff in Korea, independent of its 50-50 joint-venture refining and marketing operation with a Korean state-owned company. Though the general manager of the joint venture was a Gulf appointee, Gulf believed its own staff group could be more vigorous in representing the company with the government, especially in pressing for price increases.

When an issue crosses geographic borders but remains within

the same functional division, it is usually handled by the senior division managers. For example, the executives of the Trade and Transportation Division can quickly divert tankers or increase crude purchases in certain areas to compensate for shipping delays or supply disruptions—provided, of course, that the refineries can handle any difference in the grade of crude. In a vertically integrated network handling an undifferentiated commodity, geographic reach does not have the same *economic* importance as functional reach.

Geographic reach of issues can—and does—have significant *political* impact on operating decisions, affecting both functional and geographic divisions. The moment an upstream disruption affects a downstream operation the resolution process quickly moves beyond the division level to corporate headquarters, where it is examined for economic and political impact.

Though the primary mechanism for interdivisional coordination is the Corporate Executive Committee (or its equivalent at the top management level), oil companies often make use of informal working groups and ad hoc project teams to effect such coordination at lower levels. A good example involves a decision by a Gulf interdivisional project team to study company participation in a joint tanker venture with the Nigerian government. The government had originally requested company participation in two separate joint-venture projects in that country, the first being the tanker deal and the second, a project for the construction of a major new export refinery. On receiving these requests Gulf's local E&P managers (Gulf is a major producing company in Nigeria) sent both proposals to Division headquarters in Houston, where they were subsequently passed on to GORAM (Refining and Marketing) and the Trading and Transportation Divisions. With staff from the Science and Technology Division (which would have been involved in determining the technology aspects of the refinery project), they formed two joint project teams to consider both proposals and their wider impact on the company. After careful consideration, the groups agreed that, whereas a refinery would involve too great a financial and marketing commitment at the time, the tanker project could be more easily undertaken. These recommendations were passed on to the division Presidents.

The use of such ad hoc teams and working groups in reconciling interdivisional interests complements the formal structure and systems within divisions that are geared toward managing government issues. The observable fact across companies is that all are well prepared to resort to innovative forms and procedures when necessary.

Managing Important Issues

In a like manner nearly all company–government issues that face the international oil companies are important in their financial or strategic impact. Financially, even an "insignificant" purchase agreement from a national oil company—say, for 10,000 bb/day at $30/bb—involves a commitment of some $100 million over the course of the year. In this instance a price difference of even $.50/bb can mean a net loss or gain of $5 million before the year is out; and, strategically, the necessity to operate in a host country environment in which all issues are subject to negotiation means that government demand can have a substantial impact on future cash flows.

In terms of the overall response process, the distinction between financially and strategically important issues is significant for an oil company. Similar to the distinction between narrow and broad issues in the Assertive Mode, an issue whose importance is primarily financial is generally handled in a routine manner within the regular corporate structure of the firm; however, when an issue causes a company to rethink and reallocate its priorities throughout the system, it is generally handled by top management.

Major categories of issues that involve substantial financial commitment include new exploration and production agreements and long-term crude oil purchase contracts. The frequently recurring nature of such cases and the fact that they are generally initiated by the company means that their financial impact is adequately reflected in the budget plans and procedures for dealing with them. Strategically important issues, on the other hand, may be initiated by the host governments and may not be adequately anticipated by company plans or budgets. Examples include government demands for the renegotiation of basic operating rights and conditions, requests for participation in industrial joint ventures, and, of course, the nationalization of company operations.

An example of an issue that is financially but not necessarily strategically important can be seen in the negotiations process between Arco and the government of Dubai over new exploration and production rights. The chief negotiator for Arco, in this particular case, was the head of the E&P Division's Government Negotiations Staff. As is usual in exploration negotiations in a new country, this team included an assortment of technical specialists, engineers, and economists from the Division itself and legal and tax specialists from corporate headquarters. However, bargaining limits were defined by strict terms of reference, especially on financial matters, by senior management. In this way the involvement of top management was limited to the initial and signing phases of the negotiations.

In the case of renegotiations, however, the stakes are much more difficult to gauge. To begin with, the circumstances and facts surrounding each case are varied and need to be carefully assessed. Second, though the net result of most government-initiated renegotiations is to enhance the government's share of the pie, the *form* that different governments may wish to employ can have different implications from the company's standpoint. Whereas an increase in host-government taxes can safely be claimed as a foreign tax credit against U.S. taxes, the same cannot automatically be said of an increase in the government's share from a production-sharing agreement. All this tends to make an assessment of the economic impact of most renegotiations difficult. More important, the impact of the tenor of any response on the future climate of company–government relations and their precedent-setting ramifications needs to be taken into account. Top executives are the most logical actors who can bring to bear the global perspective necessary in making decisions on the issues involved in renegotiations.

When, in 1974, the Indonesian Government decided to raise substantially that country's share of oil company profits (including a change in the amortization method for recovering exploration costs), Arco's top management was intimately involved in making substantive decisions throughout the lengthy negotiations. The company's formal negotiating team drew on the usual division and corporate negotiations specialists and was headed by the Eastern Operating Group President, responsible for overseeing Indonesian operations. The renegotiations team reported back to top management frequently for guidance and decisions, sometimes several times during the same day. After it became apparent that the Indonesians were not prepared to relax their terms, Arco's top management decided to call a halt to all exploration activity and to reduce production.

The process followed by other companies facing the same Indonesian demands, such as Mobil and Socal, was similar. In each case senior company executives were closely engaged in substantive decision making, and, despite the fact that no specific intercompany meetings were held or agreements reached, their assessments of Indonesian terms and response choices were also similar. All companies stopped their exploration activities and cut back production.

Several months later, faced with a decline in the important Oil Reserves to Production Ratio and in the context of the increase in oil price levels during the year, the Indonesian government relaxed some of its terms. The cost recovery provisions were reinstated. Arco, still represented by the same negotiating team, also got a break in its new deals on territories in Kalimantan and the Java Sea.

The Indonesian case illustrates that even as the producing

states began asserting themselves in the 1970s oil companies have managed to retain considerable issue-specific leverage in the form of technological expertise and control over markets. Thus each negotiations process between government and firm is an individual power play.

Diversity of Response and Outcome

The centralization of decision authority in the hands of top management gives companies the advantage of speed and flexibility in responding to wide-ranging and often unanticipated government demands and requests. The necessity for case-specific decisions, however, also fosters a great variety of responses and outcomes across companies: perception of the importance of relations with a particular host country and top management personality and risk profiles may vary across companies and situations.

An example of how a difference in perception of importance can affect the process by which a company responds to a similar issue class can be illustrated by Gulf's response to the nationalization of its operations in Kuwait and Venezuela and its divestment of marketing and refining operations in Korea. Kuwait, by far the largest operation in Gulf's network, was handled directly by corporate executives at headquarters; the Venezuelan negotiations were handled tightly by senior E&P division managers. In Kuwait the company secured a major five-year, long-term supply agreement, whereas in Venezuela it settled for a "small" service-contract agreement in exchange for preferential prices. By comparison, once Gulf's Marketing and Refining division made the decision to divest from Korea, the task of negotiating a government takeover was delegated to Gulf's existing staff coordinator in that country, along with broad guidelines that permitted considerable negotiating leeway. Obviously the stakes in Korea were not deemed to be sufficiently large to require the continuous attention of senior executives. Besides, the volatile political situation following the assassination of President Park in 1979, resulting in three changes in government over a ten-month period, dictated that the case be left to people in the field who could keep abreast of developments.

The difference in company response across similar issues was even more striking in Arco's handling of the Venezuelan and Iranian nationalizations. Venezuela nationalized all foreign oil company operations in 1975. All companies were offered service contracts with technical fees and discounts on oil prices. The law required the companies to establish a guaranteed fund that would be held by the Venezuelan government until all matters pertaining to the nationalization were resolved. If the companies agreed to the compensation formula, then the compensation amount could be used as a guarantee fund. If the compensation formula was challenged, then additional monies were required for deposit into the fund. The purpose of the fund was to make sure that the company did not run down its assets and properties until it was handed over to the government. Venezuela presented Arco with a $14 million back-tax claim. If this claim was resisted, regulations required a bank guarantee for the amount of the claim, plus 110% extra for penalties and fines that could be levied on the company. Arco's top management balked at the Venezuelan terms and refused to settle on the back taxes. As a result the company ended up with its properties nationalized and nothing to show for it. Negotiations were handled by the head of the Latin American region. In an effort to expedite settlement years later in 1977 Arco established a one-person representative office in Caracas. In October 1978 a gentlemen's agreement was reached, but before it could be implemented a new government took office and the whole process had to begin anew.

Arco's reaction to the revolution in Iran was substantially different. Faced with the new government's nationalization moves, top management immediately deputed the head of the Finance and Planning Staff—an "old Iran hand"—to work out compensation and explore oil-supply arrangements. This effort was derailed by the hostage crisis that followed shortly.

The Venezuelan nationalizations also demonstrate the substantial differences in perception and response between companies in the same situation. Although major companies such as Exxon and Gulf quickly agreed to the government's terms, Arco, as noted, preferred to pull out. In this instance Arco management most likely felt secure enough with its substantive share of the Alaskan pipeline crude. With downstream operations located only in the United States and with its access to large amounts of Alaskan oil, the company was not dependent on foreign crude sources to feed its refining and marketing requirements.

The personality of top management inevitably leaves its imprint on a company's strategic moves. Arco's forceful Chairman, Robert Anderson, was the driving force behind that company's eagerness to deal with China. He openly wanted Arco to be the first to sign an exploration deal with the government and justified his position as a path-clearing move with beneficial effects for subsequent deals by other Arco divisions, such as Chemicals and Minerals.[6]

Over the many years he spent as the company's Middle East negotiator the close personal ties that Mobil's President William Tavoulareas developed with high-level Saudi officials such as Sheikh Yamani undoubtedly had some influence on Mobil's forthcoming response to Saudi overtures.

A striking example of how the differences in perception of risk and reward affect substantive decisions and outcomes across companies can be seen in the way in which Gulf and

[6]Reported in The New York Times, June 27, 1981. Arco did become the first international oil company to win China's permission to start exploration in a 3500-square-mile block in the South China Sea. The agreement was signed with much fanfare in Beijing on September 19, 1982.

Mobil responded to Saudi requests for participation in joint-venture refining and industrialization projects.

After the 1973 embargo and the nationalization of its properties in Kuwait, Gulf sent a team to the Middle East to study company opportunities in the new "postparticipation" era. Around the same time the Saudi government began to signal its intentions to embark on a large and ambitious industrialization program focusing on downstream projects such as refineries and petrochemicals. To attract foreign participation the government indicated that it would make available substantial long-term contracts on favorable terms for those companies that agreed to sign on.

Noting the Saudi proposal, as well as their own lack of participation in its lucrative market (Gulf was not a member of Aramco), the team suggested that the company follow up on the government's offer. After some initial feasibility studies a high-level delegation, including the Chairman and the President of T&T, visited Saudi Arabia, met senior government officials, including Yamani and the King, and initialed an agreement expressing serious intent to go ahead with the project. Once the letter of intent was signed Gulf expanded the small project team studying the proposal to a full-fledged Middle East Division with 40 full-time consultants, engineers, and economic and marketing experts. The creation of this division, under the charge of the former head of the Asian regional division, seemingly signaled a major corporate commitment to go ahead with the project.

In mid-1975, barely three months after the formation of the Middle East Division, Gulf suddenly decided to withdraw. The ostensible reason offered to the disgruntled Saudis was the $200-million price tag, considered too high a resource commitment in the light of the company's desire to expand its E&P operations in North America. (Gulf was also seeking diversification in other energy fields, such as coal and uranium, at the time. The total project investment was estimated at $2 billion;

Gulf's 50% share of equity amounted to $200 million; 80% of the project was to be financed by loans from the Saudi development banks and other commercial banks.)

Though cost was a major reason, several other factors contributed to the company's decision. To begin with, there was no agreement on a formula for the favorable supply of crude— primarily because the Saudis, anticipating future deals of this kind, were overly cautious about setting an unfavorable precedent. At the same time it seemed that Gulf wanted to participate in the project without putting up its own money: the company insisted that its share of the equity be initially loaned by the Saudis and subsequently paid for out of dividends, technical fees, and royalties. The Saudis strongly resisted this suggestion.

More important and subtle forces were at work in this decision than just financial consideration. About the same time this project was being considered company reorganization plans were in the offing that would change the company's structure from a geographic organization to a worldwide functional one comprised of individual "strategy centers." Project Falcon, as the Saudi petrochemical deal became known, did not fit in well with the new organizational changes: the Chemicals Division, which would have responsibility for marketing the project's chemical output, would have no bottom-line authority but was expected to accommodate the new Falcon products on a nominal commission basis. Similarly, GORAM (Refining and Marketing) would also be required to market the project's distillates on similar terms. Thus the only way that project Falcon could have gone ahead would have been if the Chairman had insisted on giving it a separate status in the new organization. As this would have affected the credibility of his whole reorganization project, he withdrew his support and the project collapsed.

The whole episode clearly tarnished the company's image in the Saudis' eyes. There was considerable resentment as to the way the project finally had been broken off (the Chairman wrote a short, but polite, letter to Yamani), and there was general agreement within the company that top management had let the issue go too far down the line before pulling back. Outside Saudi Arabia, however, there seems to have been no serious repercussions.

In contrast, Mobil succeeded because it *started* with a strategic commitment to widening its participation in joint-venture industrialization projects in the Middle East. In its 1980 Annual Report it proudly proclaimed the company's commitment to major joint ventures in ten different projects throughout Saudi Arabia, with Mobil's interests in them ranging from a 29% to a 60% equity share. The connection is clear: Mobil, as the crude-hungry partner in Aramco, saw this as a logical way to improve company access to crude supplies in the region.

At the same time and for the same reason Mobil's commitment to the Saudi government was also a pillar of top-management strategy. With a 15% stake in Aramco, senior company executives had cultivated excellent relations with Yamani and other key Saudi officials. Such was the importance attached to Saudi operations that they were managed separately from the regular functional division structure. In such a situation company divisions revolved around Saudi projects and not vice versa. For example, in March 1980 Petromin (State oil company) and Mobil signed a joint-venture agreement for a 250,000 bb/day refining complex at the port of Yanbu on the Red Sea and the following month agreed to a billion-pound/year petrochemical plant for export, also at the same location. (The trade-off in terms of incentive crude entitlements amounted to 1.4 billion barrels over a period of 19 years which Mobil began to lift in January 1981.) Yet even before the two deals were signed Mobil's Chemical Division in Europe was already expanding its capacity in anticipation of the future output of the new Saudi project.

The fact that Mobil had embarked on a strategy of collaborating with the Saudi government in large industrialization projects does not mean that the company would automatically do the same with respect to other countries or other projects.

Managing the Political Landscape

One of the interesting roles that oil companies have played, in addition to their business function, is that of transmission belts which receive and transmit messages between host and parent governments and in which senior executives are frequently involved. A classic instance occurred in May 1973 when King Faisal met with senior managers of the four companies in Aramco to pass on to Washington the Arab reactions to U.S. policies regarding Israel. In turn, the chairmen of these companies in the United States called on the State Department to communicate these messages. The President of Mobil personally lobbied the Assistant Secretary of State over the Arab anger at U.S.-Israel policy.[7]

Although the companies did not succeed in having much impact on U.S. policy ("We could always get a hearing, but we felt as if we might just as well be talking to a wall."—Rawleigh Warner[8]), they succeeded in safeguarding their own interests with host governments by showing they had tried.

More recently, alarmed by the Reagan Administration's aggressive policies toward Angola, which could lead to civil war and thus jeopardize their profitable operations, companies such as Gulf have lobbied the administration publicly and privately. Melvin Hill, President of Gulf Oil Exploration and Production, the largest oil producer in Angola, met privately with Vice-President Bush in April 1981 to urge him to revise the Angolan policy before it was too late. Testifying before the House Subcommittee, he described the Angolan government as "business-

[7]Turner, op. cit.
[8]Quoted in Anthony Sampson, The Seven Sisters (Viking, New York, 1975).

like and non-ideological, Angola has been anxious to develop an opening to the West."

Another example of how oil companies are used by host governments to pass messages on to the U.S. government in the absence of diplomatic relations involves Libya. In early 1981 Libyan officials summoned senior corporate representatives to Tripoli to urge them to use their influence in Washington to persuade the Reagan Administration to reopen the American mission which had been closed since May.

In turn, on May 7, 1981, the State Department summoned representatives of 35 companies with personnel in Libya to a conference to discuss the perils to their people there; the companies' sense of this meeting was that the State Department was attempting to send a stern message to Libya.

A case of more substantive importance, wherein the oil companies were caught in the middle, involved a decision by the IRS. The IRS found that the terms of the Indonesian production-sharing agreements negotiated in 1975 (the outcome of major renegotiations) were not acceptable as foreign tax credits, thereby necessitating a second round of negotiations between the U.S. and Indonesian governments. In this stage the companies kept a low profile; corporate lawyers and tax specialists closely monitored these negotiations.

In general, such purely political issues arise infrequently and are not so important as the substantive issues treated in the preceding discussion. However, when such issues do appear, senior company executives tend to handle them with great care and diplomacy.

GOVERNMENT-RELATIONS STRUCTURE

The formal structure of an international oil company reflects the two basic strategic imperatives of the international oil business: the necessity for vertical integration across the four basic operational phases of the industry (production, transportation, refining, and marketing) and the need for effective management of government relations at all levels.

Given the first, or economic, imperative, it is not surprising to note that five of the six companies in our sample manifest some form of worldwide functional division structure: only Exxon is organized primarily by worldwide geographical divisions. The most logical explanation for this is logistics, not politics. The sheer size of Exxon's international network allows the company to support and maintain a full complement of functional divisions in each geographic operating group. Most other companies do have geographic subdivisions within the functional divisions, though these subdivisions serve primarily as coordinating groups with little, if any, functional staff of their own. This is the case for Socal's Foreign Operations Staff, which oversees company operations in its four consortia countries, and Arco's regional divisions, which also draw from division and corporate functional staffs.

While retaining their basic functional division structure, most oil companies have addressed the rise of government power in their industry through the creation of specialized staff functions that deal specifically with government issues, the most important of which are the Government Negotiations Staffs. In some cases they have experimented with different structural arrangements such as pulling important Middle East country operations out of the formal structure and managing them separately as a group. These companies are further characterized by a centralization of decision making and tend to have well developed information systems on government issues.

The most striking feature of the formal structure of an international oil company is the existence of specialized government-affairs staffs with worldwide responsibility for the negotiation of exploration and production agreements in new countries. Members of this staff are usually full-time professional negotiators who serve as lead negotiators on the entry-level company project teams comprised of multifunctional specialists—geologists, engineers, economic analysts, and other divisional staffs.

This pattern of formalized negotiations teams allows the company to draw all relevant expertise for the negotiations process into one functional unit. At the same time, vesting worldwide responsibility for the negotiation of new E&P contracts in a central negotiating staff that is aware of past E&P contracts into which the company has entered, as well as the industry trend in general, helps to ensure that terms of any new agreements in new areas will not be out of line with existing terms. Thus this central staff facilitates the worldwide transfer of accumulated organization learning and experience from one situation to the next. The government negotiations function varies in size between 6 and 12 staffers and is usually attached to the Exploration and Production division.

The project teams include, in addition to division technical and finance staffs, corporate tax and legal staffs. It is through the latter that corporate management ensures that no significant legal issues can be overlooked. These staff units also serve as control channels for top management in major entry or renegotiation situations. Through their constant presence at these negotiations they also facilitate continuity from one situation to the next.

In the event of renegotiations the composition of the negotiating team is largely the same; however, the leadership role generally passes to the head of the geographic operating group in whose province the country is located. Once an operation is established, the operating group (or regional management) has to deal frequently with government and national oil company executives. The use of operating managers, therefore, ensures that company personnel will already be familiar with their host counterparts and be able to assess the relevant government's interests in the case. Thus it was the Eastern Region management within Arco that handled negotiations with Indonesia. Similarly, Esso Inter-America was responsible for the nationalization negotiations in Venezuela.

The process of company-government negotiations, which involves exploration and production operations, tends to be highly structured and formal. As such there are characteristic patterns of interaction between the company and host. Stoever has discussed the systematic involvement of different managerial personnel in different stages of the negotiations or renegotiations process.[9] The initial process is generally initiated by high-level executives or government officials, although negotiations-staff specialists of both company and government conduct the brunt of the detailed negotiations. Senior division or corporate executives set the terms of reference and closely monitor these negotiations but become involved only when issues defy resolution at lower levels or at the final stages of sealing an agreement. As discussed, however, division executives play a more prominent role in the renegotiations process.[10]

Other functional divisions also provide for government relations in their formal structure. For example, the Crude Acquisition Department of Gulf's Trading and Transportation (GT&T) division is responsible for all purchases from national oil companies. It, too, has a team of professional negotiators. This department is engaged in extensive discussions with various countries and is responsible for contract maintenance in countries in which Gulf has no field operations. In their constant canvassing of the world for oil supply contracts these GT&T personnel regularly monitor some 50 countries from a long-term perspective and provide a valuable source of economic and political intelligence to the rest of the organization. There is also ongoing informal coordination between GT&T staff and the government negotiations staff attached to the E&P division.

[9]W.A. Stoever, Renegotiations in International Business Transactions (Lexington Books, Lexington, MA, 1981).
[10]Ibid.

Many companies pulled important country operations, especially in the Middle East, out of the formal structure and managed them as separate operating entities reporting directly to top management. Mobil maintains a Middle East Division headed by Walter Mac Donald, who represents Mobil on the Aramco board. (Such was the importance it attached to Saudi operations that Mobil was the only oil company to name a Saudi citizen to its board.) All negotiations with Middle Eastern countries, such as Iraq and Abu Dhabi, are handled under Mac Donald's supervision with the assistance of technical and finance staff from the functional divisions.

Socal has placed four of its most important country operations under the purview of a Foreign Operations Staff at corporate headquarters. This staff of 30 persons oversees full-fledged operating companies organized in joint venture or consortia-type arrangements with other oil companies in Saudi Arabia (Aramco), Iran (the now defunct Iran Oil Consortium), and Libya and Indonesia (50-50 joint ventures with Texaco). The role of the Foreign Operations Staff is to review all matters and communications connected with these operating companies and to assist the three senior corporate executives who have been placed in charge of these four countries. These corporate executives are responsible for managing all company–government relations and for representing Socal on the board of the operating companies. As is usual in such joint ventures, there is a significant amount of intercompany negotiations among senior executives to arrive at mutually agreeable policies and courses of action. Like Mobil's Middle East Division, Socal's Foreign Operations Staff relies on other functional departments to provide technical and economic specialists in the event of actual negotiations.

Both the economic imperative of vertical integration and the political imperative of effective government-relations management necessitate some form of centralized decision making and management control in the oil industry. In an integrated network any disruptions upstream can quickly affect operations downstream, and the dominance of government power in the industry is such that companies must also be able to respond quickly and flexibly in order to achieve favorable outcomes in the negotiations process.

Thus all six companies in our sample evidenced some form of high-level management committee with major decision-making and coordinating powers. Generally, this group is comprised of senior corporate executives and division presidents.

Mobil's Corporate Executive Committee consists of 12 top executives of the company. It meets frequently, sometimes daily, to make collective decisions on most major issues. To achieve this high degree of centralization and coordination, this committee was assisted by a highly structured corporate hierarchy with well defined, sophisticated reporting and information systems.

Exxon's management committee involves the top eight executive officers of the company. Directly beneath them are the heads of the 17 staff and operating groups (one from each of the five geographical regions), the VPs of the corporate functional staff divisions (E&P, T&T, M&R, etc.), and the heads of the specialized legal, tax, finance, and public-affairs staff groups. The two fundamental parts of the organization—staff and operating group—are expected to cooperate at this level to bring geographic and functional perspectives to bear on the decision-making process. The final splicing of the two strands occurs at the top, where each of the members of the management committee oversees two or more staff and operating groups.

The extent to which authority levels are specified, and the formal chain of command, defined, is best illustrated by Exxon's capital expenditure approval process. The Investment Advisory Committee is considered to be the most important of the 17 staff functions. Unlike the others, it is headed by a member of the management committee and has substantial advisory authority over all investment proposals from the operating group heads. The strict investment approval procedures of the corporation require that any proposal between $5 million and $25 million from the operating group heads must be approved by its representative on the Management Committee and all investments of more than $25 million necessitate a full review by the Investment Advisory Committee and the approval of all eight Management Committee members.[11] This type of formalized investment review and control process can be found in all oil companies with some variations.

In Socal's management structure in the early 1980s all international roads led to George Keller, then Vice-Chairman. The Foreign Operations Staff (FOS), Chevron Overseas Petroleum, Inc. (COPI), which managed all exploration and production in the rest of the world, and Caltex, the marketing and refining joint venture with Texaco, all reported directly to Keller.

At the same time the company had instituted a special Foreign Review Committee consisting of the vice-presidents of all functional departments, the senior executives of COPI and FOS, and Vice-Chairman Keller. This committee, however, is not a decision-making body like the Corporate Executive Committee of Mobil but rather a monthly gathering to discuss and review company and political developments around the world. In the course of a typical meeting developments in Saudi Arabia and Iran were reviewed along with questions on supply for Japan. At Gulf a monthly meeting of the President's Council performed a similar function.

In dealing with government-imposed linkages across functional divisions, companies make use of ad hoc project teams of middle-level executives and staffs from the affected divisions to reconcile their joint and separate interests. Sometimes, however, the companies established formal coordinating groups to effect interaction between functional divisions or "strategy centers," and in such cases the existence of these mechanisms facilitated consideration of government issues. Gulf's Marketing

[11]A.J. Parisi, "Inside Exxon," The New York Times Magazine, August 3, 1980.

and Refining Division featured three formal groups: the Marketing Coordination Group, the Refining Coordination Group, and the Advanced Technology Coordination Group. In the 1980s Gulf began to examine seriously the possibility of offering its experimental and highly complex tar-sands technology to Venezuela to help crack the heavy hydrocarbon deposits in the Orinoco basin in exchange for the government's agreement to its equity partnership in the venture. The Advanced Technology Group was active in coordinating the technical aspects with the three divisions concerned. At the same time the presidents of these divisions were meeting to review the strategic aspects of the proposal that the company might present to the government.

In general, in considering issues involving cross-divisional linkages, such as a government request for an export refinery or a tanker joint venture, the resource commitments are so large and the strategic impact of decisions so enduring that top management or the corporate executive committee serves as the final arbiter of company response.

In terms of information flow, political and government issues are viewed as an integral part of the reporting responsibilities of operating managers. Their front-line exposure to political events and economic developments are seen as providing a realistic and timely source of information and advice on company–government relations in their areas.

This front-line expertise is captured in systematic review processes and formal reporting procedures by which regional and operating units are required to submit regular reports on political, social, and economic developments in their regions. These reports emphasize government policies and regulations that directly affect company activities. Though field reports typically concentrate on real-time events and avoid forecasting trends, some companies like Exxon require their regional organizations to express some considered opinion on various possible scenarios, especially if a high degree of uncertainty

exists, and to identify principal alternatives and their implications.

For a long-term political assessment of events oil companies
tend to have small, specialized, full-time staffs. Arco had two
full-time political analysts at corporate headquarters and two
within the International Division. Gulf had a four-man International Affairs Study unit at the corporate level. These people, in
addition to consulting with government and university sources,
also visit key countries. They are completely removed from
Gulf's operations to ensure their objectivity. Such staffs usually
prepare country profiles for top-management consideration, especially when entry into a new country is being considered.

In general, like their counterparts in Assertive companies,
these staffs operate as enclaves within the company and their
contributions to the management of government issues can be
described as marginal at best.

EVOLUTION OF GOVERNMENT-RELATIONS STRATEGIES: FROM THE ASSERTIVE TO THE STRUCTURED MODE

Anthony Sampson has described the international oil business
as:

> . . . one of the oddest stories in contemporary history: of how the
> world's biggest and most critical industry came to be dominated
> by seven giant companies; how the Western governments dele-
> gated much of the diplomatic function to them; how their con-
> trol of oil was gradually countered by the producing countries,
> until in October 1973 it appeared suddenly to be wrested from
> them. And how since then the seven companies, still the giants
> of world trade, have found themselves caught on a political
> tight-rope balancing the demands of their western oil consumers
> and their partnerships with the producers.[12]

[12]Sampson, op. cit.

For more than six decades since 1909, when the Anglo-Persian Oil Company (later British Petroleum) discovered black gold in the deserts of Persia, seven majors (Exxon, Mobil, Socal, Texaco, Gulf, Shell, and BP) dominated the world industry. In 1949 these seven companies owned combined crude oil sources accounting for 98% of the world's traded oil and most of it was channeled into "captive" downstream refineries. Formidable capital and technological barriers to entry helps explain the dominance of the "seven sisters"; but during the 1950s and 1960s the sorority was broadened by the internationalization of the smaller companies, primarily from the United States— known as the "independents." By 1970 the crude controlled by the majors had dropped to a still substantial 69% and the independents accounted for 23%. The balance—8%—was provided by national oil companies of the producing countries, a newly emergent group of actors. In the aftermath of the OPEC revolution, which saw producing countries fully flex their new found muscle, the majors' share of crude oil ownership dipped sharply to just 24% (located mostly outside OPEC); the independents' share fell similarly to 7%. National oil companies now control 69% of the world's oil supplies.

These figures illustrate the initially steady and then dramatic decline in the power of the large oil companies which have traditionally dominated the industry. Many studies have sought to examine the whys and wherefores of the rise, rule, and fall of the oil kings, thus providing a fascinating variety of perspectives to the interested reader. Here, I trace briefly the evolution of the government-relations strategies of these companies during the last three decades and examine the underlying reasons for the change in bargaining power that suggest this evolution.

It is important to note at the outset that, given the high degree of oligopolistic interdependencies between the majors and the follow-the-leader behavior that occasioned any important pricing or production decision by Exxon or BP, it is possible to speak of the evolution of these companies *as a group*. The government-relations strategies of the majors seem to have gone through three distinct phases. In the first phase, which lasted until 1970, companies routinely imposed their policies and decisions on governments. The second phase covered a brief period between 1971 and 1973 when the companies, recognizing their increasing vulnerabilities, made an abortive attempt to organize a collective, global, negotiated environment between themselves on the one hand and OPEC representing all the producing countries on the other. The third phase, commencing in 1973, represents the current strategies of companies generally striving for national accommodation. This last phase has, of course, been the main subject of our discussion.

Pre-1970: Primacy of Company Policies

Throughout the postwar period it was the companies that routinely decided among themselves the crucial questions of crude oil prices and production levels from different country sources —decisions that, in fact, determined the revenues derived by the producing country governments. Yet the latter were not even consulted on these issues!

In the 1940s host-government revenues were primarily fixed payments in the form of a royalty per barrel. In 1948 Venezuela introduced a profit-related tax based on a 50-50 split. By virtue of its simplicity this system swept around the oil world. Nevertheless, the host-government's share was calculated from the posted prices declared by the majors. Posted prices therefore inevitably became possessed of a political significance they had not had till then. In the face of the general surplus in supply that characterized the 1950s and 1960s, market prices kept declining and oil companies kept adjusting the posted price correspondingly. In February 1959 the companies effected an 18 cents/bb reduction which meant that the four major producing countries in the Middle East would receive 10% less in taxes or $132 million/year—then an enormous sum. With the oil glut continuing some 16 months later, in July 1960 Exxon's Board of Directors, on the recommendation of then Chairman Rathbone, made a fateful decision to reduce posted prices by a further 10 cents/bb—in the face of warnings from the producing countries that they would not tolerate another cut. Though executives of other companies voiced disapproval, "the sisters were all so interdependent that they all had to follow Exxon . . . the companies were solidly confronting the Middle East."[13]

This decision has been credited by many as the proximate trigger for the formation of OPEC.

Nevertheless, until 1971, despite the fact that OPEC by then had been in existence for more than a decade, the companies determined the oil revenues of host governments due to their ability to balance production rates between various major producing countries in which most were tied in intricate interlocking arrangements.

The method used by the companies in balancing production rates between countries was an ingenious one. It did not require annual or periodic negotiations among companies; rather it consisted of a secret clause (unknown to the producing country governments until 1967) written into the intercompany agreements among the participants of the Iranian Oil Consortium and Aramco. The secret "offtake agreement" (or the aggregate Programmed Quantity System) provided penalties for partners who desired more oil than a carefully calculated mean of all the partners' total demands, so that, here again, the biggest companies could set the norm for production, whereas the others would have to pay higher prices. Ostensibly, this could be justified by the larger firms on the grounds that, since each had contributed proportionately to the development costs, those wishing to take a larger than proportionate share should pay more; but in reality it was a device by which the majors could restrict their total offtake while trying to ensure that Iranian and

[13]Sampson, op. cit.

Saudi production grew roughly in line. As was to be expected, intercompany conflict was complex, for the systems mitigated against the crude-short companies. (CFP and Mobil, two such companies, were suspected of leaking the contents of the agreements.) Even after the system became known to the host governments it was not repealed; the penalties for overlifting were merely reduced. Such was the power of the majors that they were able to impose their will on host governments and on their smaller counterparts alike via an institutionalized system, thus ensuring their control of the industry.

A more dramatic case, accentuating the ability of the companies to assert their power, is illustrated by their responses to Iran's early nationalization of BP's operations in 1951. BP adopted a hard line and proceeded to enlist the support of the other majors in organizing a boycott of Iranian oil. Against the background of Anglo-American diplomatic cooperation, the other majors proved only too willing. Each had an interest in proving to the Iranians, and to other potential deviators, that they could do very well without their oil. As far as the majors were concerned, "Iran could drown in its own oil." Iran was left with virtually no access to markets. The fate of Iran was to serve as a daunting example to host countries for the next 20 years.

The Erosion of Company Power

Control of access to markets was probably the most effective leverage available to the majors—especially in a time of surplus—though not their only card. Capital, technology, and management were other important contributors to the strength and power of these companies. Over time, however, these underlying sources of strength became diluted as host governments found alternative sources for these inputs.

Since the early 1960s world capital markets, both private and international development institutions, have proved willing lenders to governments of developing countries. But more significant, and of direct consequence to the reduction of power of the majors, was the international entry of U.S. independents and state-owned companies, such as ENI of Italy, established by major consuming countries. The motivations that propelled these companies into the search for low-cost sources of foreign oil are rooted in the economic forces working toward vertical integration, though their individual timing may have been motivated by specific reasons that are beyond the scope of this inquiry. In order to gain access to oil these new entrants were willing to conclude deals that were far more favorable to host governments: governments now had more companies to choose from and could play off one company against another. It was ENI that first agreed to a joint venture with NIOC in Iran and France's state-owned group, ERAP, proved willing to operate merely as a service contractor, with no equity ownership in crude oil operations. The mere fact that the number of companies involved in exploration in the Middle East increased from nine in 1940 to 126 in 1976 increased the bargaining strength of the producing governments.[14] It gave them the option of unbundling the package of operations traditionally provided by the majors so that they could carry out some of the activities themselves, only calling in foreign help for parts that were left.

This unbundling was facilitated by the decline in industry barriers due to technology. As the technology in some stages of the oil industry matured, it became common knowledge. Examples of mature technologies abound in land-based crude exploration and production and oil refining. Oil service firms mushroomed and the process-plant contractors, such as Bechtel and Foster Wheller, were ready to provide oil refineries on a turnkey basis. To producing countries, which had slowly been developing their own national oil companies—initially as information gatherers and overseers of the activities of foreign companies—the availability of multiple sources of inputs and

[14]Turner, op. cit.

expertise induced them to participate actively in various oil industry operations. There were no insurmountable technical problems for countries to nationalize their oil industries.

Just as entry by independents and associated oil service firms reduced the majors' control of upstream operations, new entrants in downstream operations diluted their control over markets. Among European governments France, Italy, Germany, and Spain all established state-owned refining operations and reserved a portion of the local market for private domestically owned refineries. Developing countries, such as Brazil and India, also came to have state-owned refineries.[15] Japan had long had independent refiners. With the lifting of the U.S. crude-oil import quotas, the number of independent refiners looking for oil supplies increased dramatically. Although most of these independents, till 1973, relied on the majors for their supplies of crude, following the era of shortages they scrambled to strike their own deals with NOCs. By the late 1970s governments of consuming countries had joined the act. They sought bilateral deals with producing governments as a way of ensuring supplies. The national oil companies were only too eager to enter into such direct marketing deals, which by 1979 accounted for 42% of all internationally traded oil—up dramatically from just 7% in 1973.

Thus two major developments contributed to the underlying shift of bargaining power from the majors to host governments throughout the 1960s. New industry entrants in the upstream and downstream phases loosened the tight oligopolistic structure of the industry and provided multiple sources of capital, technology, and markets (albeit the latter really opened up only in the 1970s). The second development was the gradually increasing sophistication of the producing governments regarding industry affairs and their development of state-owned compa-

[15]Brian Levy, "World Oil Marketing in Transition," *International Organization*, Winter, 1982.

nies and specialized industry-oriented bureaucracies to take advantage of the opportunities unfolding before them. The stage was now set for governments to assert themselves, as they finally did between 1970 and 1973.

1970–1973: Efforts at a Collective Global Negotiated Environment[16]

In 1970, against a backdrop of buoyant oil demand, the revolutionary Libyan government acted. Carefully selecting its target, it pressured the Libyan crude-dependent company Occidental to accede to a price increase—in retrospect a watershed event that sent the oil companies on the roller coaster of ever accelerating demands from which they never recovered. In January 1971 the Gulf countries demanded price negotiations and the Libyans indicated that they too wanted further price increases. Faced with the prospect of snowballing demands, all the companies (the majors and U.S. and European independents) finally came together and agreed to a joint negotiating strategy between the companies on the one hand and OPEC, representing the producing countries, on the other. The objective: a global concordance with one set of terms to prevail for all companies and governments alike.

Predictably, the Gulf countries insisted on divorcing their negotiations from the Libyan. From the outset, therefore, the companies were forced to fall back on the concept of "separate but necessarily connected negotiations" with the Gulf countries and Libya.[17]

Having secured antitrust clearance from the U.S. authorities, the companies established the London Policy Group (LPG) and arrived at the Libyan Producer's Agreement. The LPG was a steering group of senior executives from all participating oil

[16]For an excellent account of these efforts, see Turner, op. cit.
[17]Turner, op. cit.

companies which could react quickly to new developments, provide answers to queries from the negotiating teams in the field, and modify the terms of reference for the latter as and when the circumstances dictated a change in strategy. The LPG, based at BP headquarters in London, was in charge of coordinating what were expected to be lengthy, interrelated, and complex negotiations in Tehran and Tripoli. A corresponding high-level group of company chief executives ("The Chiefs"), which met frequently at Mobil and Exxon headquarters, was set up in New York. The Chiefs met 11 times before the Tripoli Agreement was hammered out. In addition, there were numerous subcommittees to analyze technical questions and several ad hoc subcommittees to consider tax and legal issues relating to the agreements.[18]

The London Policy Group was the first government approved, intercompany bargaining forum. The companies selected the managing director of BP and the Middle East Director of Exxon as their principal negotiators. Throughout the Tehran-Tripoli negotiations the LPG met almost daily.

Initially, the LPG machinery had been meant to handle only the Tehran-Tripoli negotiations (these agreements were reached by March 1971). However, they were reactivated in response to OPEC's subsequent demands for participation in existing concessions and for upward adjustment of oil revenues to offset currency changes in 1972 and 1973; LPG was to serve as the focal institution in the industry's common negotiations in response to OPEC's demand for substantive renegotiation of the Tehran-Tripoli deal in September 1973. This time, though, the negotiations were overtaken by the Arab oil embargo—the rest is history. Thereafter OPEC countries unilaterally began to impose prices and determine production. The pendulum had swung to the other extreme.

The Libya Producers Agreement was an intercompany effort

[18]Turner, op. cit.

meant to help any of their number, should they be singled out for discriminatory production cutbacks by Libya or even outright expropriation. In essence, the companies created a safety net that committed all the companies to replace the shortfall or losses suffered by a company in resisting Libyan demands in proportion to the interest in Libyan production. A few independents did draw on the safety net as a result of Libyan sanctions, and at one point were being compensated to the tune of 650,000 bb/day.[19]

Evaluation of company efforts to seek a collective global negotiated environment is difficult. On the credit side, despite the two separate negotiations in 1971, the Tehran and Tripoli deals held in the main for more than two and a half years—by today's standards, a fairly long time. Furthermore, the fact that OPEC continued, in the person of Sheikh Yamani, to negotiate with the companies over participation and price adjustments indicates that the producing countries, too, saw merit in collectively negotiating a new international oil regime; but the effort lasted for scarcely three years, and many of the issues under consideration were left unresolved when the whole effort was overtaken by the tinderbox politics of the Middle East. How the effort might have progressed in the absence of major disruptions such as the Arab-Israeli war is now a purely academic question.

Nevertheless, some of the lessons from this era find reflection in company management of government relations today. The LPG machinery of this era may be visualized as existing in a fashion within the structure of individual oil companies. The Corporate Executive Committee, or an equivalent forum of senior executives, performs a similar function when the company is involved in major renegotiations. Another effect of this era may be found in its contribution to the cross-company fertilization of interdependent interests which helps explain the simi-

[19]Turner, *op. cit.*

larity in responses that characterize oil companies' management of government issues. As pointed out earlier, however, this similarity in company approaches was also attributable to the much longer lasting practice of country or project specific joint-venture arrangements that existed between them.

Post-1973: An Era of Mutual Accommodation

The differences in company-government relations strategies in the post-1973 period, when individual company-national government dealings once again became the norm, were notably less than their similarities. When market conditions were tight, they all conceded reluctantly to demands made by increasingly self-confident host governments. When market conditions allowed, they avoided high-priced crude and used their still substantial purchasing power (despite some reduction in their vertical integration) to try to change the quantities of oil purchased from different sources on long-term contracts.

During 1985 and 1986 OPEC faced its sternest test. Over the last 15 years the oil world had changed dramatically. In 1985 non-OPEC, noncommunist countries' production increased by 600,000 bb/day to an average of 25 million bb/day, whereas OPEC production fell 7.2% to an average of 17.225 million bb.[20] Free-world oil demand had stabilized around 44 million bb.

OPEC had had little difficulty making prices stick in the 1970s because other oil producers could not make up for the cartel's reduced output. Now that non-OPEC countries had increased production rapidly, OPEC was faced with the challenge of cutting output enough to keep prices up.

By late 1985 it was clear that the 13 OPEC countries could not muster the discipline to cut output and agree on production allocation among themselves. Saudi Arabia angrily renounced

[20]According to British Petroleum (U.K.) Annual Statistical Review of World Energy publication, reported in *Noroil*, June 1986.

its role as a swing producer and adopted a strategy of regaining market share. In October 1985 Saudi Arabia abandoned official posted prices in favor of so-called "netback deals" under which the price of crude oil was directly tied to the spot price of refined oil products.

The ensuing price war resulted in an unprecedented collapse of prices from $31 in November 1985 to below $10 in April 1986. OPEC production soared by more than 2 million bb/day, reaching a peak of nearly 20 million bb/day in August 1986. One immediate impact of this freefall in prices was its chilling affect on oil industry investments outside OPEC. In the North Sea drilling and development work slowed considerably and new work was postponed. In the United States low prices caused production to drop by 800,000 bb/day to an average of 8.7 million bb/day,[21] as high-cost marginal producers (mostly independents) were forced out of business. More importantly, shell-shocked oil companies were sharply cutting back on their oil and exploration budgets. Analysts expected that in 1986 the industry would drill fewer than 40,000 wells in the United States, roughly half the level of 1985.[22] Oil companies became reluctant to enter into contracts that committed them to buying fixed quantities of oil. In the face of tremendous uncertainty and a collapse of official posted prices, prevailing prices on the spot and futures market acquired new prominence. The oil companies welcomed netback deals in which the price of crude oil was based on what it would fetch in the market after being refined and consequently shifted the risk of price fluctuations to producers. Netback deals thus offered a protection against future losses to companies at a time of high, short-term uncertainty.

The price war also extracted its inevitable toll on OPEC. The Saudi strategy of gaining market share was a stunning success

[21]"Price Gains by OPEC Expected," *The New York Times*, February 2, 1987.
[22]*Business Week*, August 25, 1986.

but its impact on OPEC revenues was harsh. With average prices lower by 50%, total revenues were expected to be some $50 billion lower than in 1985, putting severe economic pressures on the rest of OPEC, including Saudi allies. As prices kept tumbling out of sight, OPEC was forced, for the first time in its history, to focus on its greatest weakness as an organization— the lack of a mechanism to regulate output in order to control prices. OPEC had never faced the acid test of a cartel. OPEC was now being asked to be more than just a forum for analysis and dissemination of information and a place where members met to agree on price.

Alongside mounting economic pressures, political pressures, too, were intensifying on the Saudis. Iran was a prime source. "We have made it very clear to Saudi leaders that unrestrained oil production that leads to lower oil prices amounts to a declaration of war against us," a senior Iranian official explained.[23] In the United States policy makers voiced concern over the adverse impact of falling oil prices on the domestic oil industry and the consequent slowdown in economic activity in the oil states of the Southwest. Some concern was also expressed over the threat of declining prices to the oil companies that were deeply in debt as a result of the mergers and on the ability of Western banks to collect on their loans to oil-producing debtor countries like Mexico.

By midsummer 1986 it was clear that getting OPEC's 13 price-battling members to agree on oil production controls would remain, in the words of one minister, "Mission Impossible—until we reach an agreement."[24] On August 5, 12 of OPEC's 13 members reached an agreement to reduce production by approximately 15% in September and October.[25] This deci-

---

[23]Interview quoted in The Wall Street Journal, October 31, 1986.
[24]Quoted in Business Week, August 18, 1986.
[25]Because Iran and Iraq, at war with each other, could not agree on their relative production levels, Iraq was exempted at Iran's behest in the interests of reaching an agreement among the group.

sion, by its very nature, represented a holding action. Members were unable to agree on specific country quotas or the price level that they would seek to defend. Nevertheless, it was widely viewed as the first step in that direction. On announcement, oil stocks gained 10% and oil futures contracts rose 30% over the preceding week, settling at more than $15 a barrel for the first time in months.[26]

The Iranian-Saudi rapprochement continued over the summer, culminating in a meeting between Iran's oil minister and Saudi King Fahd prior to OPEC's meeting in October 1986. At that meeting Saudi Arabia backed away from its insistence on a larger share of OPEC production immediately. In addition, it endorsed Iran's proposal for extending the general production restraint until the year end. The reversal of Saudi strategy of emphasizing market share was now complete. Final confirmation came in late October with King Fahd's ouster of the long-serving Saudi Oil Minister, Sheikh Yamani, who was most often identified as the architect of Saudi's price-war strategy. His successor, Hisham Nazer, immediately called for the OPEC countries to enforce a fixed oil price of at least $18/bb—a position that went a long way toward meeting the demands of OPEC's Iranian-led majority for higher prices.

The elements were in place for a watershed OPEC meeting in December 1986. With Iran and Saudi Arabia working in tandem for the first time in years, OPEC crafted its response to the most challenging crisis in its 26-year history. Twelve members of the group[27] agreed explicitly to defy market forces and substitute a fixed price of $18/bb starting February 1, 1987. To defend this price the OPEC producers agreed to reduce output by 7% and set specific daily production quotas for each country.[28] In addition, members agreed to phase out by the end of January all

[26]Business Week, August 25, 1986.
[27]Iraq was exempted temporarily from the agreement as a result of a compromise.
[28]"OPEC Begins New Strategy to Take Control," The Wall Street Journal, December 22, 1986.

sales contracts based on a free-market pricing of oil in favor of its fixed price structure. This amounted to a prohibition on all so-called netback deals.

Thus the stage was set for another major tussle between OPEC members and oil companies certain to resist the imposition of a new fixed price and averse to the dismantling of their netback contracts. In the words of Kuwait's oil minister, Ali Khalifa al-Sabah, "Over the next month or so, the market will test the agreement very, very hard. We shouldn't be frightened if the companies say, 'Sorry boys, we will not be picking up your crude.' They will come back soon enough."[29]

OPEC moved rapidly to win pledges of support from major non-OPEC producers. By early February OPEC had received commitments from the Soviet Union, Mexico, Egypt, Norway, and Malaysia to keep a total of about 400,000 bb of oil a day off the markets as a gesture of support.[30]

The companies were proving difficult. In the light of their experience over the last year, they were understandably reluctant to be locked into new prices for a long period. Moreover, the worldwide excess inventory of crude oil in December, estimated at some 250 million bb, was large enough to allow companies to withhold commitments to fixed-price oil for a period of several weeks and giving them time to observe and test OPEC's commitment to live up to the agreement.

The four U.S. companies involved with Aramco—Exxon, Mobil, Texaco, and Socal—were quite unenthusiastic about Saudi Arabia's offer for a five-month contract to lift a specific volume of oil at the fixed price. In recognition of their concerns Saudi Arabia had to grant the companies "wide flexibility" without any "fixed minimums or percentage limitation" on what they lift at those fixed prices.[31]

[29]*Op. cit.*
[30]"Price Gains by OPEC Expected," *The New York Times*, February 2, 1987.
[31]Quoted from the Middle East Economic Survey in "Saudi's Return to Swing Producer Role in OPEC Is Seen Sustaining Oil Price," *The Wall Street Journal*, February 11, 1987.

Thus, although the contract stipulates that the four U.S. companies would take about 1.2 million bb/day of Saudi oil till June at the OPEC fixed price of $18/bb, the oil companies can choose not to buy any oil at all, at a month's notice, if the fixed price appears out of line with free-market prices. In addition, *The Wall Street Journal*, quoting knowledgeable sources, reported that, "the companies (can) lift as little as 50 percent of the contracted volumes at any time. The net effect is to force Saudi exports up or down in defense of the fixed price."[32] Saudi Arabia was displaying its seriousness and commitment to the pact by acting as OPEC's "swing producer."

During February 1987 pressure on OPEC mounted steadily as free-market prices fell as much as $2 to 3/bb. Supply exceeded demand on world markets, partly due to cheating by some cartel members. This was compounded by excess oil company inventories. As the crisis of confidence in OPEC's ability to maintain its price and production agreement deepened, the Gulf Cooperation Council members—comprised of Saudi Arabia and five other southern Gulf producers—met in emergency session. They warned oil companies to stop playing OPEC countries against one another for price advantage and hinted at a solidarity plan to counter such moves.[33]

The Gulf Cooperation Council (in a move reminiscent of the intercompany solidarity efforts rooted in the Libyan Producers Agreement of the early 1970s) resolved to "find appropriate solutions to assist members in case it became obvious that some countries are unable to market (oil) due to company pressures that can affect the (OPEC) agreement on prices and volumes."[34]

In a veiled threat to oil companies seen as discriminating against small producers to force price concessions, Kuwait's oil minister Ali Khalifa al-Sabah warned, "If one of the international oil companies refrained from buying oil from any of the

[32]Op. cit.
[33]"OPEC Accord Coming Under Pressure as More Firms Refuse to Buy Cartel's Oil," *The Wall Street Journal*, February 24, 1987.
[34]Op. cit.

GCC countries in an attempt to pressure it into accepting a price below the official level, none of the other GCC countries will compensate the company for the lost quantities and won't sell it anything in excess of the already contracted amounts."[35]

By mid-March the oil cartel was producing only 14.5 million bb/day, 1.3 million bb below its authorized ceiling because of cuts in production by Algeria, Iran, Qatar, Nigeria, and Saudi Arabia. But the single strongest source of resistance to oil company pressures to sell oil at below OPEC's fixed price of $18 was Saudi Arabia. Saudi production had fallen to about 2.5 million bb/day, close to its lowest ever output level.[36] In addition, OPEC members were developing plans to help weaker members in the face of oil companies' efforts to test their resolve. Kuwait was preparing to market Qatar's oil through its vast network of oil refineries and distributors in Western Europe.[37] In the words of analyst Pierre Terzian, "In all its 25-year history, this episode of resistance and sacrifice is by far the strongest demonstration of solidarity by OPEC."[38]

Some seven weeks into its new agreement analysts were increasingly prepared to give OPEC the benefit of the doubt. OPEC's low production and high resolve were forcing oil companies to run down their inventories sharply. The cartel was, for the moment, displaying a remarkable degree of discipline. And one could argue that higher oil prices would benefit the oil companies' exploration and production units.

The longer term repercussions of the dramatic developments of 1986-1987 remain to be played out. The United States has once again found itself increasing its reliance on imports to make up for its loss of high-cost domestic production. OPEC had effectively conveyed the message that its members, especially Saudi Arabia and the Gulf states, controlled the lowest

[35]Op. cit.
[36]"Saudis, Front Liners in Oil Price Fight, Cut Output Close to a Record Low Level," The Wall Street Journal, March 20, 1987.
[37]Op. cit.
[38]See interview quoted in The Wall Street Journal, op. cit.

cost sources of oil. In the words of one analyst, William L. Randol, last year's turmoil "will prove in the long-run to be brilliant for Saudi Arabia and OPEC." He added, "For American energy producers and consumers, however, its long-term effects could prove to be disastrous."[39]

In the medium term crude oil production in key non-OPEC countries was expected to decline and consumption to rise for the rest of the decade, thereby increasing the demand for OPEC oil to at least 21 million bb/day by 1990.[40]

Whatever the long-term prognosis, it was clear in the spring of 1987 that the recent dramatic oscillations of the market and the ensuing tests of strength between OPEC and the oil companies would not be the last.

In search of optimal situation-specific outcomes within the broader need to seek continual accommodation with host governments, we have seen how companies have developed well defined structures and processes that will enable them to bring company and industry-wide knowledge to bear in evaluating opportunities, identifying risks, and weighing different responses in the light of evolving corporate strategies.

[39]Quoted in "Price Gains by OPEC Expected," The New York Times, February 2, 1987.
[40]Analysts' estimate reported in The New York Times, op. cit.

5
Overview and Implications

This study categorizes the strategies and behavior patterns of 13 large multinational companies into three distinctive modes of government-relations management: the Diffuse, the Assertive, and the Structured. It should be clearly noted, however, that actual behavior patterns do not fall into such neat clusters but rather stretch along a continuum from the Diffuse to the Structured with many firms combining individual characteristics of the three. The management mode under which each company is classified provides a reasonable representation of the dominant features of its approach in responding to the challenges of managing government relations.

The study provides evidence that a firm's government-relations strategies evolve as a result of a natural learning process, the diversification into salient industries, adoption of integrated strategies, and changes in relative bargaining power. Based on our analysis, certain important implications for managers and government officials are apparent.

THE THREE MODES: A COMPARATIVE ASSESSMENT

The three management modes are not presented as policy choices for company managers but rather as descriptive models of the actual behavior of the 13 firms in our sample. It is not surprising that companies new to the international scene or those that operate in industries of no particular interest to governments are most likely to fall into the Diffuse Mode simply because the costs of dealing with government issues in an ad hoc way are still less than the costs of organizing to deal with them. However, for firms in highly salient industries or for those that pursue highly integrated production strategies the opposite is generally true: they are much more likely to adopt organized, anticipatory policies and practices for the management of government relations. Structured companies, of course, engage in a continuing—and sometimes ambiguous—accommodation to government power in their industries, and adjust their strategies and structures accordingly.

Though the choice of a particular approach to government-relations management is largely dependent on specific characteristics of the industry and company, one can suggest certain specific strengths and weaknesses of each that appear to be independent of the particular reasons for adopting them.

For example, because Diffuse companies essentially deal with governments only when they must, they tend to show a limited capacity to perceive and respond to trends in government behavior. This generally results in disjointed and incremental responses as companies attempt to satisfy one constraint after another. Thus the management of government relations can quickly take on a decidedly defensive cast, often requiring crisis management as government actions begin to affect company operations.

Another weakness of the Diffuse Mode is the vulnerability

of company responses to the personalities and perceptions of front-line managers. Because there are no specific company policies or internal guidelines for dealing with governments, the resolution of important issues is often left to local managers whose more parochial concerns may compromise the wider interests of the company as a whole. This same lack of policies and guidelines also results in a propensity for issues to rise quickly through the corporate hierarchy to an overburdened top management that is forced to act as integrator and arbitrator on the entire range of government concerns, both critical and non-critical.

The strengths of an Ad Hoc Approach, implied by the Diffuse Mode, lies chiefly in its flexibility: unconstrained by any predetermined policies or guidelines, managers are frequently able to respond in new and perhaps innovative ways and, in some cases, to take advantage of opportunities that in a more tightly controlled situation would go unnoticed.

Assertive companies, on the other hand, are distinguished by a conscious and deliberate approach to government-relations management. The keystone of this approach is the negotiated environment in which companies enter into understandings that may be implicit or achieved through a constructive dialogue with host governments on issues that affect both their short- and long-term interests.

The advantages of this approach are numerous and self-evident: to begin with, an assertive posture makes possible the achievement of consistent outcomes in similar issue-areas across countries. As such, it greatly facilitates the multinational strategic planning process. It permits the firm to be responsive to government concerns while pursuing consistent strategies that are vital for integrated operations or for taking advantage of network resources and avoiding costly duplications.

An explicit policy framework, such as the clear company terms of IBM or the more flexible guidelines of Ford, serve three purposes in the management of government relations: they help to identify major government concerns and allow both line and staff managers to be aware of company positions; they signal future trade-offs that the company might offer or agree to live with; and they allow middle-level management to handle government issues while ensuring that there are no great divergences in responses across issues, thus obviating the need for top-management involvement in issues of local concern.

The a priori consideration of trade-offs across government issue-areas, inherent in an Assertive posture, permits the company to deal with issues in the early stages of the issue's life cycle. The company can present its response before an issue is politicized, with the attendant repercussions this may entail for the company-government relations in the long run. This does not, however, mean that Assertive firms eschew a conscious strategy of holding out on certain issues. On occasion, a firm may deliberately pursue a strategy of delay, ultimately preferring no agreement to an unacceptable compromise.

Government-relations management, as repeatedly noted, is a function that intimately involves line and staff managers at every level across the organization. The existence of guidelines or policies permits the explicit and extensive use of the regular structure of the firm to resolve government issues. This has the effect of expanding awareness and simplifying procedures to deal with government issues throughout the organization. At the same time, because the reach of government issues cannot be adequately anticipated, it is difficult to legislate an assignment of decision-making responsibilities or to define procedures in advance to resolve conflicts. Recognizing this, Assertive firms make wide use of extrastructural mechanisms to affect the integration of divergent interests or points of view of affected subunits and the clarification of complex issues and problems.

The use of extrastructural mechanisms permits firms to increase their decision-making repertoire. It exposes managers throughout the organization to complex trade-offs involved in most decisions and serves to develop interrelationships and communications between managers with different perspectives and at different levels that facilitate a cooperative decision-making environment. In addition, because of the considerable flexibility afforded in determining the composition, agenda, and leadership of such temporary structures, top management can easily influence the outcome of any issue by controlling the inputs into the decision process. At the same time, as vehicles for conflict resolution, extrastructural mechanisms are invaluable in their potential for providing a highly reliable and differentiated flow of information and ensuring a high degree of loyalty in the implementation of responses eventually decided on.

As regards the shortcomings of the Assertive Mode, one can point to a few key problems that might arise. To begin with, once specific policy guidelines are determined it becomes difficult to judge exactly when exceptions to policy should be made. Because any exception could potentially have a system-wide impact, significant pressures must exist for consideration of policy revisions. Since a change in policies lies in the purview of corporate top management and must be preceded by a debate within the organization, the process of revising, adapting, or changing policies can be long and cumbersome, sometimes resulting in lost opportunities.

A note of caution must also be sounded regarding the frequent practice of resorting to extrastructural mechanisms for resolving government issues affecting differentiated units. Simply using extrastructural mechanisms is no panacea: they can just as easily result in paralysis as resolution and decision making can deteriorate into horsetrading. This highlights the necessity for top-management attention to the creation of an appropriate decision environment in which such mechanisms are used. Their effective use requires that top management be involved in monitoring the quality of decision making by constantly forming, altering, and managing numerous management interactions. The challenge for top management shifts from actual decision making to one of managing the decision process or environment.

In the long run, of course, top management can broaden management perspectives and foster a cooperative decision environment by opening or creating multiple channels of communication, the creative use of manager movements and career paths, and a willingness to adapt formal systems to facilitate flexible decision making.[1]

In the Structured Mode the dominance of government power over company and industry affairs translates into the necessity for ongoing negotiations across any and all issues. In this situation the nature of outcomes depends largely on the nature of the circumstances surrounding each issue; however, by developing formal structures and processes for dealing with government issues, a company in this mode has a greater chance of capturing and using its own situation-specific bargaining power and influence at any given point.

Given the high degree of vertical integration in these companies, most government issues have a broad impact across both functional and geographic divisions. This creates a tendency toward a centralized management process as senior managers act as both integrators and arbitrators across a wide range of critical and noncritical issues. However, in recognition of the importance of the role of governments in their industry environment, an unambiguous centralization of the decision making process permits top management to ensure timely and flexible responses to government issues.

[1]For a comprehensive discussion of the elements involved in the decision-environment management mode see Christopher A. Bartlett, *Multinational Structural Evolution: The Changing Decision Environment in International Divisions*, Harvard Business School dissertation, 1979; see also C. Bartlett, *Multinational Structural Change: Evolution Versus Reorganization*, Working Paper Series: HBS 81-74, Harvard Business School, Boston, MA, 1981.

The advantages of pursuing a structured approach to the management of government relations are clear: it provides the most effective means of surfacing issues and implementing responses and the most effective guarantee that all relevant facts and opinions will be brought to bear on any given issue. In the same vein it seems to provide the greatest benefit from organizational learning.

The weaknesses of this mode, however, are also readily apparent: first, as in the Diffuse Mode, the centralization of power can easily result in the overburdening of top management (which, likewise, can leave the company vulnerable to the personalities and perceptions of a few top managers), and, second, it creates a distinct potential for conflict within the company, with opposing viewpoints so clearly defined and articulated that all affected parties know exactly where the trade-offs lie and, consequently, who will be helped or hindered the most by any decision handed down from top management.

As indicated at the outset, a multinational firm is not equally likely to adopt one of the three modes of government-relations management. Rather, as the three preceding chapters have shown, depending on its characteristics, a firm is more likely to favor one approach over the others.

FACTORS INFLUENCING GOVERNMENT-RELATIONS MANAGEMENT

In Chapter 1 three major factors were postulated as influencing the specific choice of government-relations strategy and management mode adopted by a firm. These factors were defined as the *salience* of the particular industry, the overall company *strategy* pursued, and the *spread* of international operations. Based on our analyses, it is possible to evaluate the importance of each of these factors.

The most important is clearly the salience of the industry concerned: the more important an industry in the government's eyes, the more frequent and encompassing the range of government issues with which the firm must deal and the greater the constraints arising from political, as opposed to economic or market, criteria. Industries deemed to be important by governments usually include those that are major revenue producers or employers or are considered leading industries of the future. As managers of the national economy, government officials focus their attention on these industries in their quest to ensure growth in incomes and jobs, development of the national technological infrastructure, and favorable trade balances. Companies operating in salient industries cannot avoid addressing government demands—and, indeed, all such companies in our study pursued either Assertive or Structured approaches toward government-relations management. As such, salience appears to be a *sufficient* condition for the adoption of an organized, anticipatory approach to managing government relations.

Clearly the degree of salience varies across industries. Industries in which governments exercise significant power over resources (such as oil) or markets (such as telecommunications and drugs) may be rated as having higher salience than other sectors, such as computers or autos, where no such power exists. In the industry sectors that fall within the higher range of salience governments tend to develop specialized departments or bureaucracies for overseeing industry affairs that in turn will greatly influence the specific strategy and structural choices of the firm. For example, both Eli Lilly and ITT have developed matching company specialists to deal with specific government pricing, licensing, and purchasing bureaus or agencies. The oil industry, of course, illustrates the extreme end of this continuum: the company organization hosts a bevy of specialized structures whose prime concern revolves around government relations.

Although salience appears to be a sufficient condition for a firm to pursue an Assertive or Structured approach to government relations, the specific approach adopted requires a careful analysis of the nature and degree of salience and the relative bargaining power of the company vis-à-vis the government (the latter is more fully discussed in the next section). At the same time it is important to note that salience does not appear to be a *necessary* condition for a firm to be an Assertive manager of government relations. A firm operating an integrated network of subsidiaries may well develop an anticipatory approach to government issues, even though it operates in nonsalient industries.

Overall company strategy is another important factor affecting the choice of government relations strategy. The key elements here are the degree of integration across national borders and the consequent interdependence among the various subsidiaries in the company's network: the more integrated the network, the wider the impact of any one government demand, and the more significant the precedent-setting impact of any one company decision. Moreover, in an integrated company most government demands must be dealt with centrally because the very interdependence of its subunits requires a certain consistency of response and outcome across issues. Clearly such challenges are of less significance to firms that pursue other (less integrated) strategies.

Based on this study, the existence of an integrated strategy appears to be a *sufficient* condition for the adoption of an Assertive approach to government-relations management; however, as in the case of ITT—an Assertive company with a clear, country-oriented strategy to overseas operations—it does not appear to be a *necessary* one as well. In ITT's case salience is a governing factor. Correspondingly, one can point to companies that are integrated but not assertive, as in the case of Xerox, which, despite its extensive network of integrated operations, remained essentially Diffuse until the late 1970s. At the same time, however, one can suggest that integrated companies are most likely to develop more Assertive approaches in order to avoid the inevitable costs of reactive management with their disruptive systemwide effects. Again, Xerox serves as a prime example.

In the treatment of company strategy as an independent factor influencing the mode of government-relations management a key assumption is that a company has the flexibility to choose or adapt the broad dimensions of its overall strategy along a fairly wide range. Government actions, however, can influence or constrain the choices of strategy open to a firm. It is important, therefore, to note the feedback effects of government policies on company strategy.

In general, without any government intervention, MNCs could reasonably be expected to pursue global strategies that draw on a common pool of resources and skills to maximize their competitive advantage. They would tend to operate in ways that take advantage of economies of scale and maximize the synergy among affiliates. However, government policies designed to influence foreign subsidiaries to respond to national goals and objectives force MNCs to effect a variety of compromises, adaptations, and changes in their strategy. At the extreme, in highly salient industries (typically characterized by high government power), company strategy may be influenced in a fundamental and deterministic way in the direction of country-oriented, nationally responsive subsidiaries. Such adaptation in strategy is most likely to occur in the manufacturing sector in which a prime purpose of a subsidiary is to serve the needs of the local market. In the natural resource sector, on the other hand, the prime function of this subsidiary is to serve the international market by the export of raw materials and the scope for such fundamental adaptation of strategy is not great. Even in the natural resource sector, however, national responsiveness is reflected in the variety of *forms* that have been developed for conducting local operations (such as management contracts and production-sharing agreements) that give the impression of greater national control.

As noted in Chapter 2, ITT's adoption of a country-oriented strategy was itself a reflection of the dominant role of governments in the telecommunications industry. Even when company strategy is one of nationally responsive subsidiaries, multinational companies retain some sources of strength (such as new technologies or channels for exports) that are viewed as contributions to the local economy. Were this not the case, governments would probably encourage a local takeover. Takeovers are most likely to occur when a subsidiary is self-sufficient and derives little or no advantage from being part of the multinational network.

The spread of a firm's network of operations also has an impact on the costs and benefits of government-relations management. The larger a firm's network, the more opportunities it has to harness its experiences and to apply its learning from one situation to the next. Moreover, the larger the spread, the higher the costs generally associated with inconsistent responses to similar government demands. This study confirmed our expectation that the larger the spread of a firm, the more it is driven toward developing an organized approach to government-relations management.

It is difficult, however, to come to any unequivocal conclusions about the importance of spread per se. This is because the influence of spread, as an independent factor, tends to be mitigated by the extent to which it is correlated with the other two independent factors—namely salience and strategy—or dominated by them. In our sample companies with large spread also tended to operate in salient industries and/or pursued integrated strategies. There were no cases of a company that had a large spread and was nonsalient and nonintegrated at the same time. Because the influence of spread cannot be determined independently of the influence of salience and strategy, no conclusion regarding sufficiency can be made. However, spread appears not to be a necessary condition because counterfactual cases were encountered. A firm can be in a salient business or pursue an integrated strategy (each satisfies the sufficiency condition) and have only a small network, yet be an Assertive or Structured company. (Arco and Conoco are two examples.)

Spread does seem to encourage the development of internal capability to transfer experience and knowledge, thus helping to speed up the natural learning process of a company in overseas markets. As such, it appears to be an independent factor of secondary importance to this study.

It may be appropriate to note here a few research avenues that this study provides. Within MNCs it would be interesting to examine the differences in government-relations strategies and management practices across companies in the same industries. This would permit a better appreciation of the factors that determine the approach that a company will adopt. By holding salience constant one can evaluate the importance of strategy and spread. Another direction might be to investigate the government-relations strategies of MNCs in Europe and Japan that are products of more symbiotic relationships between their home governments and themselves. Does this give them an edge?

EVOLUTION OF GOVERNMENT-RELATIONS MANAGEMENT: PATTERNS OF CHANGE

A company can move from one mode to the next as circumstances change and old solutions become outmoded. The very dynamism of the international government-relations environment demands an equally dynamic ability to respond across issues. Xerox's experiences and the history of government-relations strategies of oil companies reveals that there are definite patterns of change and distinct factors that trigger movement and specifically influence company choices as they evolve from one mode to the next.

The discussion in Chapter 3 of the transition from the Diffuse to the Assertive Mode, as reflected in the Xerox case, revealed a distinct pattern of change. In response to a series of serious government-relations problems in the mid-1970s the company designed and implemented an information-gathering system that could raise company awareness and permit an anticipatory response posture toward government issues. However, it was not until Xerox began to diversify into a more salient industry sector that it seriously began to consider a more assertive approach. A similar process of change was noted at both Cummins and International Harvester. At Cummins the natural process of learning and adaptation was telescoped into a very short period by the impact of a few closely spaced government-relations crises, whereas at Harvester serious attention to government issues seems to have begun only after the company had instituted a significant organizational change that further integrated company operations across national borders.

Thus, in tracing the transition from the Diffuse to the Assertive Mode, one can distinguish three distinct patterns of change: diversification into salient industries, the adoption of more integrated strategies, and a natural learning process often telescoped by a government-relations crisis. In each of these patterns the underlying dynamic, of course, is the growing realization by the company of the power and influence of governments on their operations. In the transition from the Diffuse to the Assertive Mode key business decisions can no longer be viewed with sole reference to the marketplace but are elevated to the more complex arena of business-government interface; in such a situation the continued reliance on ad hoc policies and practices is simply poor management.

Thus one can conclude that any factor that increases the importance of the company in the government's eyes or the government in the company's eyes will occasion some internal movement toward a more assertive approach to government-relations management.

Once in the Assertive Mode, however, the dynamic changes.

The key question becomes one of how to manage the interface effectively. As discussed in Chapter 2, there are three distinct approaches that make up the continuum in this mode: the policy-oriented "pure-type," which is characterized by the ability to impose company policies and self-developed trade-offs on host governments as a condition for operating in national markets, the more flexible policy approach that emphasizes the initial entry-level negotiations with host governments, and the more stuctured, nationally accommodating approach in which governments control key sectors of company operations or retain sufficient market power to be able to dictate terms. (This range of three distinct management approaches within the Assertive Mode itself illustrates the strength and the messiness of this analysis.) Exactly which particular combination of assertive policies and practices a company will choose is clearly dependent on how effectively it is able to make its case and press its claims against the growing power and influence of governments in its industry. This, in turn, is fundamentally related to the underlying bargaining strength of the company vis-à-vis the government.

Bargaining power is thus the central dynamic of the Assertive Mode: the progression from IBM's centralized policies to ITT's national accommodation strategies is clearly an adaptation to the gradual (or, in some cases, abrupt) decline in company bargaining power at the company-government negotiating table. Vernon has labeled this phenomenon, "the obsolescing bargain."[2]

In attempting to explain the progression along this continuum it is useful to analyze the fundamental sources of bargaining power for the company, namely capital, management skills, technology, and access to markets. Because capital and management skills are generally available on an unbundled basis, their relative bargaining value decreases as governments

[2]Raymond Vernon, *Sovereignty at Bay* (Basic Books, New York, 1971).

continue to locate independent sources. The same is not necessarily true, however, for technology and market access: here the real threat to company bargaining power comes from other competitors, not government demands (this does not preclude governments from using them to play one company against another). With reference to competitors in the industry, a combination of all four factors provides the basis of a firm's competitive advantage. In terms of a firm's relations with host governments, generally only access to technology and markets define the "renewable" or proprietary sources of bargaining strength available to a company in its bids to remain and prosper in the national economy.

In light of this analysis, the transition process within the Assertive Mode itself can be described as the outcome of the extent of decline in the control over sources of capital and management skills versus the continued importance of technological innovation and geographic diversification in maintaining a competitive advantage. It is control over the latter aspects that permits some companies to undertake country-oriented strategies, yet be classified as assertive managers of government relations. Companies like ITT are able to offer host governments a nationally responsive subsidiary designed to cater to the needs of the individual national markets as well as significant access to overseas markets and the benefits of a coordinated and varied R&D network. In return they seek to ensure continued preferential treatment by the government-owned PTTs that dominate the industry markets.

The obsolescing bargain concept can also be analyzed from the government's perspective. The power of governments increases as a result of their increasing knowledge of and sophistication in industry affairs often reflected in their development of specialized organizations to deal with foreign companies in those industries and the increase in the number of global competitors within the industry itself, giving them more options from which to choose. These factors clearly came to prevail in the Indian electronics industry before the Indian Government finally forced a confrontation with IBM.[3] In this context it is interesting to speculate how IBM would respond if other, more important, national governments, such as Brazil and Mexico, were to press their claims. Would IBM withdraw as it did in India or would it consider a more flexible policy approach in which it would seek an explicitly negotiated understanding specifying mutually acceptable trade-offs? Surely at some point the cost of losing important markets will become greater than the cost of a directly negotiated environment, even though this may mean some compromise in its tightly controlled, integrated network. Of course, IBM can continue to hold the governments of advanced countries at bay as long as it retains a significant technological lead.

In a similar vein one can speculate about the situation Ford will face in the future when it can no longer undertake massive new investments to strike long-term understandings with governments. Having already engaged in the practice of actually negotiating trade-offs and entering into direct terms with governments, it is likely that Ford will be able to cope without great trauma under less favorable circumstances. To be sure, Ford may be required to negotiate and renegotiate agreements for shorter periods of time and the degree to which commitments are specified may be more detailed. Consequently Ford may have to develop more specialized structures and supporting systems for handling this kind of an ongoing situation; but this transition will probably not involve as great an adjustment as the prior set of conditions might for IBM.

Two more observations on the patterns of change within the Assertive mode:

First it is important to note the increased importance of management mechanisms as one progresses along the continuum

[3]Joseph M. Grieco, "India's Experience with the International Computer Industry," *International Organization*, Summer 1982.

from the policy approach to the more structured, nationally accommodating approach. Once the substantive superiority of a
company weakens, success in the international market becomes
increasingly dependent on the ability to coordinate effectively
and integrate similar activities across a broad network of subsidiaries.[4] Companies must be able to develop a repertoire of
management mechanisms and tools that will allow them to involve subsidiaries in strategic decision making while at the
same time controlling their activities. The second observation
concerns the direction and reversibility of evolution in government-relations management. Our discussion has been concerned with the transition from power to weakness within the
Assertive Mode, but given the right circumstances the progression can occur in the opposite direction as well. Though we
have no specific examples in our sample we can easily postulate scenarios, such as a company developing a significant technological breakthrough in a salient industry or a government
deciding to pursue a policy of liberalization in business sectors
important to multinational companies to see that companies
can sometimes (though not quite so easily) enhance their bargaining power and as a result change their specific approach toward government-relations management.

The transition from the Assertive to the Structured Mode
government-relations management has also been analyzed at
some length in our discussion of the recent history of the international oil companies. Here the role of bargaining power is
again the central dynamic: over the last 15 years oil companies
have gone from a highly assertive, policy-oriented approach to a
highly structured mode of managing government relations. In
terms of our analysis of the specific sources of bargaining
power, we can describe a structured company as one that has
lost substantial—or retains little—control over the proprietary

---

[4]Yves Doz makes this point in *Multinational Strategic Management: Economic and Political Imperatives*, draft, 1980.

sources of renewable strength in its industry. As our best example, the oil companies have seen not only their control over capital and management skills diminish but in significant measure their control over technology and markets as well.

What kinds of companies might evolve along the progression from the Assertive to the Structured Modes? Within the Assertive Mode even those companies that were forced to accommodate significant government demands in vital areas of their business were still able to retain a decisive measure of control over their markets and technology. If this were not the case, one could safely assume that there would no longer be any reason, in the eyes of company management or government bureaucracy, to stay in business.

This does not, however, seem to be the case among the oil companies. Despite the dramatic increase in government control and ownership in recent years, as the analysis of Chapter 4 clearly points out, companies can still bring to bear significant situation-specific bargaining strength. This suggests the presence of certain qualitative differences in the sources of bargaining strength affecting both company and governments, such as the international demand and supply situation at a given time and the wishes of home (and consuming country) governments.

In times of glut the power of the oil companies is higher because their established marketing channels permits them to use this leverage to entice preferential terms from eager suppliers. In times of shortage the opposite is true. Further, oil companies will continue to play a significant role in oil exploration, production, and marketing in the liberal economies of the industrialized countries and in new oil-producing developing countries. As long as the U. S. and European governments continue to rely on these companies to service their markets, the governments of mature producing countries will have to continue to deal with them. In addition, oil companies are valued providers of technology and management skills for industrialization projects that the major producing governments are eager to undertake.

A combination of these factors indicates the rationale for developing a highly structured approach to government-relations management involving continuous negotiations on a wide range of issues. It also suggests that companies in only a few industry sectors are likely to cross the threshold into the Structured Mode and maintain a viable position once they get there. One can readily point to other extraction or natural resource industries that share the quality of high salience combined with the influence of situation-specific bargaining power. Guyana was able to nationalize ALCAN and other aluminum companies in the early 1970s because of its being the world's major source of calcined bauxite. Guyana thus felt it could do without the marketing network of a vertically integrated company. Jamaica's levy of a production tax was resisted, however, and the government was forced to lower the tax as companies increased production elsewhere at Jamaica's expense.

To be sure, in no other extractive industry is the power of host governments as great as that in oil. An educated guess might suggest that resource-based companies are likely to be more structured than assertive in their approach toward managing government relations.

This discussion has highlighted the key role played by bargaining power in the choice of government-relations strategies. Company management would do well to reevaluate their bargaining strengths and competitive advantages periodically and to assess the implications of any changes on their postures toward government-relations management.

IMPLICATIONS FOR MANAGEMENT

Managing government relations is still a largely undefined area of management practice. Although some companies have been developing innovative strategies and approaches for dealing with governments, they know very little of what other firms are doing. Yet other companies are struggling to evolve their own approaches in an era when government actions show an ever-increasing tendency to impinge on business operations. Managers find that in a large number of decision areas they need to take into account the government implications of any decision. This study will have achieved its major objective if it enables managers of multinational firms to understand and benefit from the experience of others.

Clearly it is difficult to evaluate the performance of a firm's government-relations management per se. There are numerous questions as to what constitutes performance in this ill-defined and all-encompassing function. Against what criteria should performance be measured? Across what time horizon? Whose performance can and should be measured: that of the firm as a whole or those of its different subunits? How can one differentiate the contributions of different line and staff managers toward government-relations management? Finally, because the acid test of performance lies in outcomes and the variables affecting outcomes are seldom entirely within the control of managers, can a fair and equitable assessment of performance be made?

This research focused on developing an understanding of a firm's approach to government issues as a whole and on examining the factors that drive firms to adopt particular approaches. Given this broad research objective, the thorny questions posed in the preceding discussion were not addressed directly. Rather it was assumed that if a firm pursued a consistent government-relations approach for a period of time then that firm felt its extant strategy was appropriate for its own particular circumstances. If the influence of the major characteristics or factors motivating firms to adopt a particular approach could then be assessed, this analysis could be used by other managers who are placed in similar circumstances. If a manager whose company shares common characteristics with some firms described here finds that his company's practice differs markedly, he or she may be able to assess fruitfully whether the company could benefit from altering its approach to the management of government issues. By carefully assessing the relative strengths and weaknesses of different modes, for example, the management of an integrated firm whose approach toward government issues is still reactive can assess its costs against the potential benefits of organizing to deal with government issues.

This research has also served to highlight the importance and possibility of consciously integrating government issues in choosing overall company strategies and designing organization structures and administrative systems. There will, of course, always be some multinational companies for whom the cost of managing government relations may be higher than the cost of seeking ad hoc solutions. On the other hand, the Exxons and Mobils will continue to expend considerable resources in developing and maintaining structures and systems for dealing with national governments.

For a majority of multinationals, however, the optimal choices are likely to lie somewhere between the extremes. For this large group of multinationals the impact of government relations on the profits of a firm and its inherent demands on the top management are discussed next and some guidelines are suggested to show how firms may develop a government-relations capability within their organizations.

Managing Government Issues: An Activity With Significant Impact on Profits

Reginald H. Jones, former Chairman of General Electric Company, epitomized the importance of government relations in these words:

> We have found over many years that the key to business success in any country is to consult with people who are there, both the officials in charge of economic policy and the private sector people. . . . Find out what they are trying to do—their priorities, their plans for the nation, their most urgent needs, their rules for

participation in the local economy. Then figure out the best way to make your capabilities and products and services fit their needs and regulations. If a company takes the trouble to do this groundwork, then the odds are in favor of business success because both parties—the company and the host country—*want* the venture to succeed. Relationships between companies and countries do not develop suddenly. . . . Usually it's an evolutionary process.[5]

Government requests or demands pose significant problems for multinational managers. However, they often provide significant opportunities as well. Governments that seek local R&D facilities or greater exports are also likely to provide substantial subsidies or grants as inducements. Governments that insist on higher local value-added also routinely provide a protected market environment. More generally, many governments exercise considerable influence on the allocation of credit through the financial system and some state enterprises enjoy considerable market power by virtue of their purchases. In such cases the management of an MNC can gain access to scarce resources or extract substantial benefits in return for being nationally responsive.

Governments are equally prone to using the "stick" as well as the "carrot" to induce responsive behavior. A 5% reduction in transfer price may very well wipe out all the productivity improvements for which an operations manager may have striven long and hard. A "temporary delay" in import licenses for a vitally needed component can bring local production to a halt. And there is a variety of other administrative measures that governments can employ whose impact, although less dramatic, is no less costly to the multinational firm.

An anticipatory, organized approach toward managing government relations by systematically appraising the opportunities and risks may make a significant contribution to a firm's success and profitability. To be sure, the benefits of a govern-

[5]Cited in *Harvard Business Review*, November-December 1980, p. 155.

ment-relations program may not be directly measurable. For example, the usefulness of a manager's efforts at developing good personal relations and credibility with local government officials, although difficult to measure, may explain why that firm received preferential treatment or avoided a particular problem. Over the long run management of government relations can magnify the impact of traditional sources of competitive advantage and indeed provide one itself.

Despite the clear—and often inevitable—imperative of dealing with government issues, some U. S. executives are wary of the notion of government relations. Having grown up in an environment in which business-government relations have traditionally been at arms-length, these executives have difficulty accepting the concept of a negotiated environment involving understandings with different governments. This attitude breeds the policy, "deal with governments only when you must."

This view boils down to considering government relations only when a company seeks protection or needs to be rescued by the government or when it must defend itself against threats or actions by government officials.

The realities of the international environment today require a broader and more informed view of government relations. In most countries, including the industrialized states of Europe, governments view their role as national economic managers as a legitimate activity. For the managers of most multinational firms this fact of life dictates that government relations be viewed as a legitimate activity that needs to be actively managed and can significantly affect the firm's international competitive posture and profitability.

Government Relations Is a Top-Management Activity

Management of government issues demands close top-management involvement in policy formulation and implementation. Scholars have long ascribed an institutional role to top management, one that involves the acquisition and maintenance of legitimacy bestowed by governments and other societal elites.[6] However, there are also strategic and operational reasons demanding top-management involvement in government relations. To begin with, senior executives are often the only ones who can bring to bear a systemwide perspective to the assessment of the trade-offs involved between alternative courses of action and their implications for different subunits within the firm. As decision makers who can control and commit a firm's resources, they are often required to represent the firm in important negotiations. This is reinforced by the fact that in many countries there is a long tradition of centralized authority. Senior executives are better able to secure access to the centers of power in the government.

To recognize the necessity for top-management involvement in government relations is not to imply that they should be involved in substantive decision making. The sheer volume and frequency of government issues, with the attendant risk of information overload, may dictate otherwise. Rather top management can instigate and direct a debate on government issues among managers at all levels with the objective of increasing awareness and developing policies. Further, top management can establish or specify organizational mechanisms by which various government issue-areas can be handled and internal conflicts resolved. By including government-relations management as a parameter in the firm's measurement and reward system top management can help instill a continued sense of the importance it places on this activity. By thus influencing the decision environment within the firm corporate management ensures that most government issues are handled by the relevant country or division managers, thus enhancing the credibility of the latter in the eyes of government officials.

[6]J.J. Boddewyn's "Multinational Business-Government Relations: Six Principles for Effectiveness" in *Multinational Corporations and Governments*, P. Boarman and H. Schollhammer (Eds.) (Praeger, New York, 1975).

Internal Policies on Government Issues

A company can benefit greatly by explicitly considering the whole range of issue-areas that is likely to be involved in company-government relations. What is crucial to the development of an anticipatory approach is to set out company objectives across issue-areas considered as a whole, recognizing that compromises in some areas are inevitable and necessary in order to address government concerns. Only by considering the full range of major issue-areas together can a company develop a fuller perspective of the options for compromise available to it. It permits companies to specify issue-areas in which they are willing to compromise and the extent of such compromises that they find tolerable.

Xerox's approach focused on surfacing issues early and identifying the priority issues at each review stage, thus enabling responses to be formulated in an anticipatory fashion to potentially important problems. Only the highest priorities were dealt with thoroughly. At the other extreme a firm may devote special attention to a single issue-area, unconsciously relegating or ignoring the importance of others. In one firm, for example, a senior executive proposed and secured the establishment of a task force on the question of "national demands for greater local value-added." The four members of the task force spent the better part of a year discussing this issue extensively with major subsidiary, area, and product division managers. Although this exercise may have served to increase awareness within the firm on this single area, it is hard to see what kinds of meaningful recommendations it could have yielded. If a wider range of issue-areas had been considered, the company could have decided that its integrated strategy would be better served by promising governments that the company would maintain a trade balance as opposed to making any specific commitments on local value-added.

The nature of trade-offs a company may choose to make depends on the characteristics of the company. A drug firm pursuing an integrated strategy might emphasize its adherence to uniform transfer pricing worldwide but shirk any commitments on local value-added, whereas another drug company pursuing a country-oriented strategy may stress its willingness to undertake or expand local operations but may follow differentiated transfer pricing policies designed to reduce taxes and duties.

The benefits of an internal policy framework for the management of government relations are obvious and have been discussed at length in the first section of this chapter. The process of developing this framework, however, requires widespread internal debate and takes time. But it is time well spent. Companies that have undertaken this exercise typically have formed task forces at various levels comprised of both line and staff managers to discuss the relative importance of various issue-areas and different trade-off options. Developing a consensus at a time when the company is not beset by a major government-related crisis and no subunits feel specifically threatened ensures an atmosphere in which overall corporate interests might prevail.

Management of Extrastructural Mechanisms

In the comparative assessment of the three different modes the benefits and difficulties of employing extrastructural mechanisms to effect lateral communication links and as conflict resolution forums for managing broad government issues were discussed. Here the considerations on assigning managers to such mechanisms to ensure their effective use are presented.

Possibly the most important consideration is that all managers whose interests are affected should be included. This ensures the legitimacy of the group and provides for the differentiated information inputs and perspectives that bear on the problem at hand. Managers whose commitments are required in the implementation phase should also be included.

By itself, however, even this may not ensure joint problem solving. To avoid paralysis or horsetrading top management might wish to pay attention to the careful assignment of leadership roles in using these mechanisms. Attention needs to be paid to the power and status of the leader and the other managers on the team. It helps to select a leader who is highly regarded by the major affected units and who are in some fashion dependent on him. At the same time the leader must bring to bear a corporate perspective as he guides the team toward a "consensus decision."

Adaptation of Administrative Systems

A company can ensure adequate and continual review of government issues by making sure that they are considered as part of the administrative systems such as resource allocation, strategic planning, performance evaluation, and information systems.

The company resource allocation system, for example, may provide the setting for extensive intersubsidiary communication and consideration of each other's plans or treat each subsidiary independently. It may require explicit consideration of the costs and benefits of a companywide plant in one location versus a series of national plants. The strategic planning process may be used to force recognition of potential interdependencies or joint costs among several of the firm's subsidiaries or businesses or to stress the autonomy of the subsidiaries.

Few companies have made a systematic effort to develop performance objectives in the government relations area for their managers. This is due primarily to the inability to specify meaningful objectives in terms of results to be achieved because outcomes are not necessarily within the control of country managers who might be held responsible. Yet there are creative and flexible ways of including government-relations objectives in the manager's performance evaluation. Even if the objectives specified are more process- as opposed to result-oriented, the inclusion of such objectives as part of the firm's regular measurement system provides a strong and visible mechanism for affecting the orientation of country managers. One company even included broad government-relations objectives for their regional managers. For example, the President of the Middle East Division was charged with "taking steps necessary to remove the company from the Arab Boycott List." In general, the inclusion of government-related objectives in a line manager's evaluation ensures that operational considerations do not dominate and drown government-relations management. It is also a powerful means of forcing managers with narrow country or product perspectives to adopt a broader corporate viewpoint.

Finally, the information systems of a company may require country managers to provide constant updates on their experiences in the government-relations area, and this information can be disseminated across the organization to enhance knowledge transfer. By periodically requiring country managers to present their perspectives on government issues before their peers at companywide conferences or meetings top management can signal the importance they attach to them on an ongoing basis and encourage interpersonal communication between managers whose interests might be affected by a given government issue.

In introducing these changes, top management should not expect an immediate turnaround in the orientation and behavior of country and division managers. Basic attitudes do not change overnight. Rather adaptations to administrative systems should be viewed as the starting point of a process of change.

If, for example, country managers are given additional responsibility for government relations, they will legitimately expect that their recommendations be given due weight. Top management should make sure that powerful staff groups at corporate or area headquarters understand this and establish a

dialogue with country managers to arrive at mutually acceptable decisions. Country managers should be given extensive
feedback on how their analyses and recommendations influenced the eventual decisions. When they are overruled, the reasons should be clearly explained. It is only through such a process that country managers will begin to develop confidence
that their recommendations will be taken seriously and that
they have acquired an important say in the decision-making
process.

In order to change staff orientations top management should
emphasize that managing government issues is important to the
success and profitability of the firm and the contributions that
knowledgeable country managers can make in that process.
This can be done by seizing on government-relations crises that
the company may have experienced recently and highlighting
what went wrong and the consequent costs to the firm. Further,
involving representatives of staff groups in periodic discussions
of government issues will serve to drive home their roles and
responsibilities in the process.

Clearly there are significant costs in seeking to introduce
a government-relations capability within an organization. For
many firms, however, the sustained benefits of such a formal,
systematic consideration of government issues promises to be
great, far exceeding short-run adjustment costs.

Role of Specialized Government-Relations Staff

The most striking aspect of the existence of a so-called government-relations function or staff is the wide differences in the interpretation of this function and the role of this staff in different
companies. The uniform result for most companies is the marginal or insignificant nature of the contribution of this staff to
the actual management of government relations as defined in
this study.

A major reason for this lies in the diversity of roles assigned to this staff and the kind of people employed for this activity. In many companies the nomenclature "government-relations staff" applies to a group of political scientists assigned to developing broad environmental or country surveys. This group often operates as an enclave within the firm, isolated from the rest of the organization by a lack of any significant appreciation of the industry and operational significance of the macro trends they study so carefully.

Yet other companies have defined the role of this staff more broadly. They are viewed as advisors to senior management on major international government issues and provide a functional perspective on them. Few companies have gone beyond that to involve a specialized staff function in the decision-making process on the major government issues that concern the line managers in the firm. IBM, a major exception, provides its area external-affairs staff access to the regular business reports sent from the subsidiaries and extends to them a right of review and protest on affiliate plans as part of its nonconcurrence conflict resolution system.

A government-relations staff can play a valuable role in systematically collecting and disseminating the information, trends, and experiences of various subsidiaries to other units within the organization. In this role they can establish their usefulness to line and other functional managers. They could always be fruitfully employed in following emergent global government issues such as the transborder data flow regulations evolving in European and other industrialized countries— issues whose collective implications can best be assessed by a central corporatewide staff.

However, for a staff to be able to perform these meaningful roles it must include people with some line experience. Certainly the senior staff should have had substantial line responsibility. Only in this way can it appreciate the line manager's perspective and responsibilities and orient itself appropriately to serving the line function. Further, by doing so the government-relations function significantly improves its acceptability to line executives.

IMPLICATIONS FOR GOVERNMENTS

As Vernon has emphasized:

> More than ever before, governments are telling the affiliates of MNCs what they must do or not do as the price for the right to continue in business. . . . The various sovereigns direct their commands at the unit in the MNC; the unit responds as it can, giving ground to the sovereign if it must; the other units in the network adjust their operations to the new situation, spreading the adjustment costs through the global system.[7]

Vernon's concern, of course, is mainly with the implications of how MNCs are being used as principal weapons of many governments for pursuing a "begger thy neighbor" economic policy. He takes the same set of concerns that formed the subject of this research but poses a different central question: how do the sovereign states propose to deal with the fact that so many of their enterprises are conduits through which other sovereigns exert their influence? This question may be too ambitious to be answered at the present time, but a study of how and to what extent governments are organized to deal with MNCs may be of more tangible interest.[8]

Although this study has focused exclusively on company perspectives toward dealing with government issues, a few implications can be drawn that might interest government officials.

Probably the most important lesson for governments to bear in mind is that companies do not operate as monoliths that perform large actions for large reasons. Rather they are composed

[7]Raymond Vernon, "Sovereignty at Bay Ten Years Later," *International Organization*, Summer 1981.
[8]Professors Louis T. Wells, Jr., and Dennis Encarnation at the Harvard Business School are conducting a study on this subject.

of different organizational units with different interests and different perspectives, much like governments themselves. Often, however, government officials act as if they were incognizant of this reality. This can result in costly misunderstandings and delays that can sour company-government relations. By recognizing how the interests of different subsidiaries diverge, host-country officials can gain a better understanding of a company's vulnerabilities and the areas in which they can apply pressure effectively.

By the same token governments should realize that a company team that may arrive to negotiate with them may represent some interests and not others. Therefore the message they may wish to communicate may not get through. If a government wishes an issue to be promptly and seriously considered by the company, it should raise it at the particular managerial level that is able to evaluate it in a larger perspective. Government officials often assume that a communication with the country manager will result in the automatic elevation of the issue to the appropriate level. This study suggests that this assumption may not be valid.

Government officials should also learn to appreciate the influence of company strategy and its relation to how the company itself might approach them. If a company pursues an integrated strategy and seeks long-term agreements, then the government should insist on securing detailed and specific performance requirement commitments at the time an agreement is struck.

Finally, governments should note that different companies within the same industry may be willing to offer different trade-offs. Because a government may attach greater weight to the achievement of some objectives over others, it should shop around for a firm willing to subscribe to those conditions. This firm may be smaller or a less well known, but what it is willing to offer in local responsiveness may be of greater benefit to the national economy.

Index